# 101 sandwiches

101 sandwiches

A collection of the finest sandwich recipes from around the world

Helen Graves

DOG 'n' BONE

Published in 2013 by Dog 'n' Bone Books
An imprint of Ryland Peters & Small Ltd
519 Broadway, 5th Floor,
New York, NY 10012

20–21 Jockey's Fields,
London WC1R 4BW

www.rylandpeters.com

10 9 8 7 6 5 4 3 2 1

Text © Helen Graves 2013
Design and photography
© Dog 'n' Bone Books 2013

A CIP catalog record for this book is
available from the Library of Congress
and the British Library.

ISBN: 978 1 909313 16 3

Printed in China

Editor: Anne Sheasby
Designer: Alison Fenton
Photographer: Stephen Conroy except
pages 11, 15, 21, 67, 107, 111, 137
by Rob White

For digital editions, visit
www.cicobooks.com/apps.php

ACKNOWLEDGMENTS

I would like to thank Pete at Dog 'n'
Bone Books for finding me and for
recognising that sandwiches are ACE.
Thank you also to Donald for his appetite,
his support, his advice, and his ability to
keep me sane. Finally, thanks to mum
and dad, for making sure the fridge was
always so well stocked with things to
put between bread.

CONTENTS

INTRODUCTION

Welcome to the world of sandwiches! The humble sarnie, sanger, butty, bap, whatever you want to call it, is one of the most versatile, convenient, and popular meals in the world. I will be your guide on this tour of the best examples ever created and I am well qualified to do so, since I am a sandwich addict.

My obsession began at a young age when I would construct ideal, dream sandwiches in my sleep, only to wake up grasping at the air above me pointlessly, trying to reach out and touch my tasty creations. The fanaticism continued into teenage years as I entered a phase of building absolute monsters (very much à la Dagwood on page 105), using whatever my unwitting parents thought they had safely stashed in their refrigerator. It all went in: cold cuts, cheeses, garnishes, relishes, mayo, scallions (spring onions), pickled onions, anything. Nothing was safe. This, of course, led to some major disasters, but it was an important sandwich learning curve and laid the foundations for a lifelong love.

I think it's important we start by laying down some ground rules for when it comes to making, buying, eating, and defining sandwiches, starting with the absolute basics.

So what exactly is a sandwich? At first, this question may seem ridiculous, but actually I've encountered strong opinions about what does and what does not constitute one. Obviously, a filling between two slices of bread is a sandwich. What about a burger though? Or a wrap? And let's not even get started on the "open-faced sandwich." Okay let's. This, in my mind, does not really qualify. If it did, then surely we could call everything on toast a sandwich? Beans on toast would be a sandwich, as would mushrooms on toast, spaghetti on toast... well just about anything on toast, basically. Or is it the toasting of the bread that disqualifies "stuff on toast" from the sandwich category? Perhaps only untoasted bread can make an open-faced sandwich. Everything else I'm prepared to let in to the sandwich fold. Wraps, kebabs, burgers, even hot dogs; as long as they involve a filling wrapped, clamped, or, indeed, sandwiched, in some sort of bread.

There are some basic rules one must adhere to when making a sandwich, and yet there are some sandwiches that break them all. Let's take a simple ham and tomato filling as an example. Every sandwich should be constructed with proper care, attention, and love. The bread must be fresh and of good quality; there is a time and a place for cheap "plasticy" bread, but it is rare and should be kept that way. In the case of the ham and tomato, I'd go with a very fresh farmhouse white. Then there's the butter, which must be at room temperature and therefore spreadable; there is nothing (nothing) more rage-inducing than tearing a hole in the bread because the butter is too hard. The quality of the fillings is obviously of paramount importance; the ham must be proper cooked ham, thickly sliced off the bone (none of that shiny, "reformed" rubbish), and the tomato must be perfectly ripe and fragrant. If lettuce is to be added, then this should be used as a barrier betwixt bread and tomato; the structural integrity of the sandwich must always be preserved, and that means avoiding placing tomato next to bread if at all possible. One runs the risk of inducing sogginess as tomato juice slowly soaks into the bread; it is one of the most unpleasant and unfortunate events in the sandwich world. If there is no lettuce or the sandwich contains just tomato, then consumption must be immediate. And what about cutting? In half? Into quarters? Fingers? Triangles or squares? Crusts on or off? All these questions before we've even considered different types of bread.

White; whole-wheat (brown or wholemeal); whole-grain (granary); ciabatta; bolillo; telera; focaccia; flatbread; pita bread (pitta); roll; sub; mo; tortilla; hot dog bun; burger bun; brioche; baguette; bagel; rye; sourdough; challah; mantou; the list is long and many of the breads just listed can be found in this book, while there are still many more to enjoy. Fillings are just as numerous, but what you will find within these pages are established sandwiches from around the world; some are classics and fairly ubiquitous, while others, I'm hoping, are completely new to you. Rest assured, however, that somewhere in the world, each of these sandwiches is celebrated.

So which are the sandwiches that break all the rules? Well, there are those that are entire stuffed loaves, like the Pan Bagnat (page 94), there are those that are completely "drowned" in sauce, like the Torta Ahogada and the Francesinha (pages 75 and 34), and then there are those that are just plain outrageous, like the Luther Burger (page 35). With the Luther in mind, let's consider some of the world's freakiest sandwiches. There have been many weird and (occasionally) wonderful creations. The "fool's gold loaf," for example; there is no recipe for it in this book, but that's not necessarily a bad thing. This sandwich you see is quite the monster. A whole loaf of bread is hollowed out and filled with an entire jar of peanut butter, an entire jar of grape jam and 1lb (450g) cooked slices of crispy bacon. Woah. Apparently, Elvis was a fan, which is hardly surprising considering the loaf is stuffed with his favorite sandwich fillings (see The Elvis on page 98). The fool's gold loaf is by no means the most excessive sandwich, however. That title must go to the world's longest sandwich—a world record-breaking Mexican "super torta," which weighed a whopping 1543lb (700kg). You can make the more modest version using the recipe on page 20.

It's not just excess that defines a sandwich as outrageous however; what about the issue of "double carbs"? I'm talking sandwiches like the Chip Butty (page 31) or the Vada Pav (page 22). It's hard to believe, but some people are genuinely against the idea of double-carbing, believing it to be in some way "wrong." This is nonsense. Are they suggesting we forgo the pleasure of freshly salted and vinegared chips, hot and crisp, layered onto thick white bread and smothered with brown sauce, steak sauce, or ketchup? Are we to deny a filling a place in a sandwich simply because it doesn't fall into the category of vegetable or protein? My point is that exclusivity in the sandwich world should not be tolerated, which reminds me to mention my disdain for the habit of creating the "world's most expensive sandwiches"; part of the appeal of the sandwich is that it is a foodstuff accessible to all. I firmly believe it should remain so.

There are plenty of places to buy sandwiches, but not all those places are "safe." The hierarchy of sanger-purveying outlets goes something like this: at the bottom, we have the roadside gas stations. These places are the absolute pits, selling only over-chilled, pallid bread that sticks to the roof of your mouth, and bland watery fillings of consistently crappy quality. These kinds of sandwiches have seen the steady demise of once great fillings such as coronation chicken; sitting on a shelf for a week in something called an "artificially protected environment" doesn't do food any favors, funnily enough.

Next up, we have the convenience store sandwich, only marginally better than the gas station because, well, I'm not entirely sure actually; perhaps those two should be on a par. The supermarket or grocery store offerings are generally dismal too and... oh dear, we're not doing very well so far. The point is that, until fairly recently, a sandwich grabbed on the go was a very sad affair; a desperate act born only out of an instinct to survive and a lack of all other options. The situation improved slightly with the chain sandwich shops, though they're far from perfect, even if the sandwiches are supposedly made "fresh every day."

Then we arrive, finally, at the only acceptable options: the posh deli or purpose-built sandwich shop, or the street food stall; which is the current popular option. Traders compete at the curbside to sling the best steamed pork belly rolls, sizzling chorizo on ciabatta, or fried chicken and coleslaw subs. The options are increasingly global in flavor.

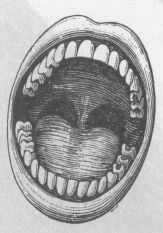

So, before we begin our journey examining some of the best sandwiches from around the world, let's consider the first. At least, the first sandwich that ever went on record.

It is commonly reported that John Montagu, the 4th Earl of Sandwich, invented the concept when he found himself hungry at the gambling table, but was reluctant to leave his card game; he therefore instructed one of his minions to bring him some meat between two slices of bread. The first sandwich on record, however, actually came much earlier, around the 1st Century BC. Stick that between two pieces of bread and slice it. Sandwich may have given his name to this most wondrous of portable meals, but he was by no means the first person to come up with the idea.

That was Rabbi Hillel the Elder, and his purpose was rather more serious. Intended to symbolize the suffering of Jews, the sandwich was to be eaten at Passover, and consisted of a mixture of chopped apples, nuts, spices, and bitter herbs placed between "matzah" (thin bread). The Hillel sandwich is rather different today, with the apple replaced by roast lamb topped with horseradish.

So, taking Hillel's sandwich as our inspiration, our archetypal sandwich number one so to speak, here's a collection of another 100 all-time greats. We'll travel through perennial classics; the realms of guilty pleasure; the most luxurious and decadent; the world's best street eats; curry and spice; summer and BBQ classics; well-connected sandwiches associated with famous characters and important people of the world; sandwiches that are real "projects" and can take a whole day (at least) to make; sandwiches born out of making use of leftovers and, finally, some sweet things. Phew!

I truly hope you enjoy the journey discovering these most excellent of sandwiches. Let's give them the respect they deserve!

CHAPTER 1 • THE CLASSICS

BLT

The combination of bacon, lettuce, and tomato has been a popular sandwich filling for donkey's years, but the combination really took off after World War II, when ingredients like tomatoes became available in stores year-round. It's debatable as to whether or not this is actually a good thing—tasteless, anemic tomato anyone?

Today, the BLT sandwich is as ubiquitous as tuna mayo or ham and cheese, and is available in restaurants, bars, cafés, and even (shudder) supermarkets and service stations. The best BLTs are, of course, made at home; preferably with a raging hangover.

Makes 2

INGREDIENTS

6 slices (rashers) thick-cut smoked bacon

2 slices thick-cut white bloomer bread

Mayonnaise

Lettuce—Boston lettuce or butter lettuce (Little Gem) is a good choice, as it has a lovely crunch, but any lettuce will do

1 ripe tomato, sliced

Black pepper, to taste

Preheat the broiler (grill) and cook the bacon until the fat is nice and crisp.

Assemble the sandwiches by spreading 2 slices of bread liberally with mayo, then add a layer of lettuce, followed by 3 pieces of cooked bacon per sandwich, and finally the tomato slices.

Season with pepper, add the final slices of bread, and serve while the bacon is still warm.

5 WAYS TO PIMP YOUR BLT:

- Make it a BLAT by adding sliced avocado.
- Add some thinly sliced scallions (spring onions).
- Spice it up with a few drops of hot chili sauce.
- Fried green tomatoes are a popular BLT addition stateside. Dredge green tomato slices in flour, then dip in beaten egg and finally in polenta. Fry on both sides until golden and add to your BLT.
- If your hangover is particularly bad, add a fried egg.

Let's lay down an important theme from the start: the huge amount of rivalry when it comes to claims of sandwich invention. The origin of falafel is one of the most hotly disputed of them all, although it is thought they were invented by the Christian Copts of Egypt, who were not permitted to consume meat during certain holidays. Falafels filled the gap. They swiftly gained popularity in the Middle East, and were particularly adopted by Israel as a symbol of national identity. Don't be tempted to use canned beans for this, they're too mushy. Don't say I didn't warn you.

Falafel Pita Bread

To make the falafel, place the garbanzo beans (chickpeas) and fava beans (broad beans) in a large bowl and cover with about three times their volume of cold water (they will swell enormously overnight). The next day, drain them and place in the bowl of a food processor along with all the other ingredients (except the vegetable oil for deep-frying). Blend until well mixed, but the beans still retain some texture.

Pour some vegetable oil into a deep frying pan or an electric deep-fat fryer and heat to 350°F (180°C). In the absence of a special falafel shaper (no, I don't have one either), it's best to shape them by hand. Take a small handful of the falafel mixture and squeeze it in your fist until it holds together. Repeat until you have used up all the mixture (to make about 40 falafel). Carefully drop the balls into the hot oil and cook in batches for a couple of minutes, until golden brown all over. Drain on paper towels. Keep warm in a low oven while you cook the rest. Serve hot.

To make the tahini sauce, mix together all the ingredients, plus some salt and pepper, taste, and then add more tahini, lemon juice, or yogurt as necessary.

To assemble each sandwich, lightly toast a pita bread and cut it in half lengthwise, leaving 2 canoe-shaped pockets. Stuff each with a little shredded cabbage, some falafel, a drizzle of tahini sauce, a pickled chili, and some pickled turnip. Enjoy while fresh and hot!

Makes enough for a small army—about 40 falafel; 8–10 servings

FOR THE FALAFEL:

2½ cups (500g) dried garbanzo beans (chickpeas)

3⅓ cups (500g) dried split fava beans (broad beans)

6 scallions (spring onions), chopped

2 tsp sea salt

1 tsp black pepper

2 tsp ground turmeric

4 tbsp finely chopped fresh flat-leaf parsley

2 tsp cayenne pepper

2 tsp ground cumin

2 tsp ground coriander

4 garlic cloves, peeled

3 tbsp all-purpose (plain) flour

2 tsp baking powder

Vegetable oil, for deep-frying

FOR THE TAHINI SAUCE:

1 heaped tbsp tahini, or to taste

1 tbsp lemon juice, or to taste

3 tbsp plain yogurt, or to taste

Pita breads, shredded cabbage, pickled chilies, and pickled turnips, to serve

Makes 4

INGREDIENTS

FOR THE CARROT AND DAIKON PICKLE:

½ cup (125ml) rice wine vinegar

1 tsp sea salt

¼ cup (50g) superfine (caster) sugar

1 carrot, about 2¾oz (75g), cut into short thin sticks

1 daikon radish, about 7oz (200g), cut into short thin sticks

FOR THE CARAMEL PORK:

6 tbsp superfine (caster) sugar

1¾lb (800g) pork belly, skin removed and cut into cubes

Scant ½ cup (100ml) fish sauce (Three Crabs is a good brand)

4 scallions (spring onions), white parts only, bashed with the flat side of a knife

2 garlic cloves, peeled and bashed with the flat side of a knife

4 black peppercorns

A pinch of sea salt

4 x 6in (15cm) (-ish; don't go getting the tape measure out) lengths of white baguette

Mayonnaise

1 fresh red chili, sliced (seeded or not is up to you)

1 cucumber, halved and sliced lengthwise into long sticks

Fresh cilantro (coriander) leaves

The bánh mì is arguably one of the world's greatest sandwiches. A light baguette is stuffed with various fillings, which may include pork, pâté, sausages, sardines, or tofu, among others. It is garnished with fresh cilantro (coriander), chili, cucumber slices, and pickled carrot and daikon radish and is a lesson in the power of contrasts.

The sandwich is a product of the French colonial presence in Vietnam, which resulted in ingredients like baguette, mayonnaise, and pâté being combined with Vietnamese pickles and spice.

Caramel Pork Bánh Mì

To make the carrot and daikon pickle, mix the vinegar, salt, and sugar together in a bowl until everything is dissolved. Add the vegetables and press down to make sure they are all covered by the liquid. Set aside to pickle for at least an hour before eating, or a couple of days (in the refrigerator) if you're feeling organized. The pickle will keep for around 4 weeks if well sealed and stored in the refrigerator.

To make the caramel pork, mix the sugar with 4 tablespoons water in a pan and cook over a high heat, without stirring, until the sugar is a rich golden color. Very carefully add the pork cubes to the pan and stir so the meat is coated with the caramel. Add enough water to cover the pork, then slowly bring to a boil, skimming off any impurities that rise to the surface.

Reduce to a simmer and add the fish sauce, scallions (spring onions), garlic cloves, peppercorns, and a pinch of salt. Cook, uncovered, for 15–30 minutes, or until the pork is tender.

Remove the pork from the liquid and set aside on a plate. Remove the scallions and garlic cloves from the liquid and discard, then turn up the heat. Let this reduce until you have only ½in (1cm) or so of liquid left—this should take about 10 minutes. Place the pork back in the pan and stir well.

To assemble the banh mi, split each section of baguette and hollow each piece out slightly by removing some of the bread inside. Spread one side with mayonnaise and add a few slices of fresh chili. Add some caramel pork belly chunks, followed by a heaped tablespoonful or so of carrot and daikon pickle, some cucumber sticks, and cilantro (coriander) leaves. Serve immediately.

The Reuben

As already noted, when something turns out to be incredibly popular, several people often want to step in and take the credit for it. Funny that.

First up to claim the title of Reuben Creator is Lithuanian grocer Reuben Kulakofsky, who is said to have invented it during a card game. His fellow competitor Charles Schimmel then put the sandwich on his hotel menu and it quickly shot to fame on account of its extreme deliciousness. Not having any of that, though, is a guy by the name of Arthur Reuben, who founded Reuben's Delicatessen in New York. He is said to have cobbled the sandwich together when an actress unexpectedly visited the deli requesting something substantial to eat. A third claimant to the title was a dude named Fern Snider, who is said to have entered it into a sandwich competition (and won).

Whatever the origins, this is a world classic among sandwiches; a true belly-stretching behemoth to be found in good Jewish delis, or... made at home using this recipe. It's a monster, packed with as much salt beef as you can handle, Swiss cheese, sauerkraut, and Thousand Island dressing, all on toasted rye.

Makes 1

INGREDIENTS

2 slices light rye bread

Butter, at room temperature

2 tbsp Thousand Island dressing

2 tbsp sauerkraut, well drained

2 slices good-quality Swiss or Gruyère cheese

4–5 thick slices salt beef, with lovely wobbly fatty bits if possible

Heat a frying pan. Spread both slices of bread with butter on one side only. Place 1 of them, butter-side down, on the pan. Spread 1 tablespoon of the Thousand Island dressing onto the dry side of the bread. Make sure the sauerkraut is well drained, then add this to the slice of bread, followed by the cheese and then the salt beef.

Spread the remaining dressing on the dry side of the remaining slice of bread and add it, dressing-side down, to the sandwich. Press down several times. Carefully turn the sandwich over and weigh it down by placing a heavy pan on top. When the sandwich has turned crisp and golden brown on the bottom, flip it back over for 30 seconds or so, to make sure the other side is properly heated through. Serve immediately.

English Tea Sandwiches

The daintiest of all sandwiches are those served at afternoon tea. We can thank the 7th Duchess of Bedford, Anna Maria Stanhope, for their invention; she hit upon the idea of nibbling a light morsel to see her through from lunch to the evening meal, which in those days (mid-1800s) wasn't eaten until 8pm.

Whether tea sandwiches are cut into fingers or triangles is entirely the choice of the maker, but one thing is certain—they should always, always have the crusts removed.

Egg and Cress Finger Sandwiches

Makes 6

INGREDIENTS

2 cold hard-boiled eggs

1 tbsp mayonnaise

1 tsp snipped fresh chives

3 pinches of salad cress

Sea salt to taste and a pinch of white pepper

4 slices white bread, thinly cut

Peel the eggs, mash them with a fork, then stir in the mayonnaise, chives, and salad cress. Season with salt and the white pepper. Spread the filling onto 2 slices of bread, then top with the remaining slices. Remove the crusts and cut into finger sandwiches. Serve immediately.

Radish and Anchovy Butter Finger Sandwiches

Makes 6

INGREDIENTS

3 canned anchovy fillets, drained

1 tbsp (15g) butter, at room temperature

4 slices white bread, thinly cut

5 radishes, very thinly sliced

Finely chop the anchovies and then use a fork to mash them into the butter. Mix until really well combined. Spread 2 slices of bread with the anchovy butter, then add a layer of radish slices on each. Top with the remaining slices of bread, remove the crusts, and cut into finger sandwiches. Serve immediately.

Cucumber Finger Sandwiches

Makes 6

INGREDIENTS

¼ cucumber

Sea salt, for sprinkling

Lemon juice, to taste

4 slices white bread, thinly cut

Butter, at room temperature

Score the skin of the cucumber lengthwise with a fork so that it is stripy in appearance. Halve it, then scrape out the seeds with a teaspoon. Thinly slice the cucumber, then put the slices in a colander and sprinkle with salt. Set aside for 30 minutes to drain. Sprinkle over a little lemon juice and mix well.

Spread each slice of bread thinly with butter, making sure to spread right to the edges. Add a layer of cucumber slices to 2 of the slices, then sandwich together with the remaining slices of bread. Remove the crusts and cut into finger sandwiches. Serve immediately.

Dill, Shrimp, and Egg Smørrebrød

As mentioned in the introduction to this book, the definition of what equals a sandwich and what does not can be a contentious issue. The smørrebrød, a Scandinavian "open sandwich" is just such a classic, however—I feared the prospect of hate mail from angry Scandinavians if I had not included it.

The smørrebrød (pronounced 'smurd-a-bra') is basically a slice of buttered, dark rye bread, which is then used as a base for a tower of different toppings that may include (but are not limited to) pickled herrings, smoked salmon, meats, cheeses, vegetables, red onion rings, and thick, remoulade-style sauces.

Originally found hiding in lucky workers' lunch boxes, topped with home-cooked cold cuts, the smørrebrød was adopted and adapted by society's elite, who piled them high with extravagant ingredients. There are many possible combinations but one thing is constant— the smørrebrød should always be too pretty to eat. Almost.

Makes 1

INGREDIENTS

1 slice dark rye bread

Butter, at room temperature

1 cold hard-boiled egg, peeled and sliced

10 small cooked peeled shrimp (prawns)

1 tbsp mayonnaise

A small sprig of fresh dill, finely chopped

A squeeze of lemon juice

Sea salt and black pepper, to taste

A little salmon roe, to serve (optional)

Spread the rye bread with butter and top with slices of egg. In a bowl, mix the shrimp (prawns) with the mayonnaise, dill, and lemon juice, to taste. Season with salt and pepper and then pile onto the smorrebrod. Top with a little salmon roe, if using.

Serve immediately with a glass of chilled schnapps, aquavit, vodka, or ice-cold beer.

Katsu Sando

This Japanese sandwich contains the wondrous creation that is tonkatsu, a breaded, deep-fried pork fillet or loin. Japanese panko breadcrumbs coat the outside, forming a super crisp exterior and preserving the juices of the meat within. The tonkatsu is sandwiched between white bread and garnished with shredded cabbage, mayonnaise, and tonkatsu sauce, which is basically like a sweet curry sauce.

It is a sandwich of wonderful contrasts, as all great sandwiches are: the soft white bread against the sizzling fried pork cutlet, the sweet and spicy tonkatsu sauce... my stomach, it growls.

Start by giving the meat a good bash with a rolling pin to tenderize it and ensure that it is the same thickness all the way through. It should be thinner as a result. Spread some flour on a plate and dip the pork chop into it, covering both sides. Next, dip the pork chop in the beaten egg, then in the panko breadcrumbs, until it is evenly coated all over.

Pour some vegetable oil for deep-frying into a deep frying pan or an electric deep-fat fryer and heat to 350°F (180°C). Deep-fry the coated pork chop for about 6 minutes, turning occasionally, until golden brown all over and cooked through. Drain on paper towels.

To assemble the sandwich, spread 1 slice of bread with mayo, then slice the deep-fried pork chop and lay it on top. Add a generous drizzle of tonkatsu sauce, followed by some shredded cabbage and the second slice of bread. Guzzle the deep-fried wonder that is the katsu sando.

Makes 1

INGREDIENTS

1 pork chop, bone removed

All-purpose (plain) flour, for dusting the pork chop

1 egg, beaten

Panko breadcrumbs, for coating

Vegetable oil, for deep-frying

2 slices white bread

Mayonnaise

Tonkatsu sauce (available from Asian supermarkets)

⅛ napa (Chinese) cabbage or green (white) cabbage, finely shredded

The Mexicans are very proud of their tortas, which sounds like a euphemism but isn't; I refer to their celebration of this gut-busting sandwich. Every year they pay homage by holding a festival in Mexico City; such dedication to the sandwich should be admired.

It is possible that the first torta was eaten during the French occupation, when Mexicans took inspiration from the baguette and used a similar recipe to create telera and bolillo rolls. They're stuffed with different combinations of ingredients depending on the region (see Torta Ahogada on page 75), but whatever your preference, the fillings absolutely must be many in number. Layer and garnish to your heart's content. Buen provecho!

Mexican Torta

Makes 2

INGREDIENTS

2 cooking chorizo sausages

2 tomatoes, diced

½ red onion, finely chopped

1 lime

1 tsp chipotle flakes, or 1 chipotle chili, finely chopped, or 1 fresh red chili, finely chopped

About 1 heaped tbsp roughly chopped fresh cilantro (coriander)

Sea salt and black pepper, to taste

1 avocado

2 Mexican rolls such as bolillo or telera, or 2 lengths of soft-ish white baguette, or 2 ciabatta rolls (hardly authentic, the latter, but sturdy enough to contain all that filling)

2 tbsp canned refried beans

Set a frying pan or ridged griddle pan over a medium-high heat. Split the chorizo sausages in half lengthwise, place them in the dry pan, cut-side down, and cook until crisp and beginning to char. Flip them over and cook the other side.

Meanwhile, make a tomato salsa by mixing the diced tomato and red onion with the juice of ½ a lime, the chipotle chili, and cilantro (coriander). Season with salt and pepper. Halve, pit (stone), and peel the avocado. In a separate bowl, mash the avocado and mix it with a squeeze of lime juice.

Cut the rolls in half and lightly toast them. Dip the cut side of each roll into the chorizo pan, to coat with some of the chorizo fat that has leached out during cooking. Spread one half of each roll with a layer of mashed avocado, then add the chorizo sausages. Top with the tomato salsa. Spread the other half of each roll with the refried beans and use them to top the sandwiches. Serve immediately.

5 WAYS TO TART UP YOUR TORTA:

- Add cooked chicken or, better still, smoked chicken.
- Add a crumbly white cheese, such as feta cheese or queso fresco, if you can find it.
- Substitute the chorizo sausages for 2 sirloin steaks (each about 4½oz/125g).
- Add a fried egg for a breakfast torta.
- Blend a couple of chipotle chilies in adobo sauce and use as a spread in place of the tomato salsa.

INGREDIENTS

FOR THE SPICED POTATO MIXTURE:

2 fresh green chilies, finely chopped (seeded or not is up to you)

1 garlic clove, crushed

Thumb-sized piece of fresh ginger, peeled and grated

2 tbsp vegetable oil

1 tsp black mustard seeds

A pinch of asafoetida (optional)

10 (fresh or dried) curry leaves

1lb 2oz (500g) cold mashed potatoes

½ tsp ground turmeric

Sea salt, to taste

4 tbsp chopped fresh cilantro (coriander) leaves

Vegetable oil, for deep-frying

FOR THE SWEET CHUTNEY:

6 dried dates

½ tsp tamarind purée

FOR THE DRY GARLIC CHUTNEY:

10 garlic cloves, peeled

1 tbsp peanut (groundnut) oil, plus extra for frying

½ cup (35g) dry unsweetened (desiccated) coconut

1 tsp chili powder

FOR THE GREEN CHUTNEY:

A large bunch of fresh cilantro (coriander)

A handful of fresh mint leaves

About 5 fresh green chilies, chopped (seeded or not is up to you)

Juice of 1 lemon

1 tbsp vegetable oil

FOR THE BATTER:

Generous 1 cup (100g) chickpea/besan (gram) flour

¼ tsp ground turmeric

A pinch of baking powder

Scant ⅓ cup (80ml) water

5 soft white rolls, split open, to serve

Fried fresh green chilies, to serve (optional)

Vada Pav

Of Maharashtrian origin, the vada pav is a very popular Indian street food snack, consisting of spiced deep fried potato, garnished with various chutneys. The credit for invention often goes to a man named Ashok Vaidy, who slung his wares from a stall outside Dadar station in 1971. Beats a soggy sandwich on the train home from work, huh?

To make the spiced potato mixture, mash together the chilies, garlic, and ginger. Heat the vegetable oil in a pan, add the mustard seeds, and cook until they pop. Add the asafoetida, if using, and the curry leaves and cook for 10 seconds. Add the chili/ginger paste and cook for 10 seconds. Add the mashed potatoes, turmeric, and salt, then add the cilantro (coriander) and mix well. Remove from the heat and let cool.

Meanwhile, make the chutneys.

To make the sweet chutney, soak the dates in warm water for about 20 minutes, then remove the pits (stones). Whizz the dates in a blender with the tamarind purée and a splash of water to form a tomato sauce-like consistency. Set aside.

To make the dry garlic chutney, gently caramelize the whole garlic cloves in a frying pan with a little peanut (groundnut) oil. Add the coconut, stirring until golden. Blend together with the chili powder and the remaining 1 tablespoon peanut oil. Season with salt. Set aside.

To make the green chutney, blend the cilantro, mint, green chilies, and lemon juice together with a splash of water. Add the vegetable oil, plus some salt, and blend to mix. Set aside.

To shape and cook the potato mixture, pour vegetable oil for deep-frying into a deep frying pan or an electric deep-fat fryer and heat to 350°F (180°C). Shape the spiced potato mixture into balls (to make about 20 balls).

To make the batter, mix all the batter ingredients together, then dip each potato ball in the batter. Deep-fry the balls in batches for about 6 minutes, turning occasionally, until golden brown all over. Drain on paper towels. Keep warm while you cook the rest. Serve hot.

Serve the warm potato balls in the white rolls with the chutneys and fried green chilies, if using.

The mantou is a cloud-like steamed bun or roll, which floated all the way from Northern China. The origin of the word "mantou" is attributed to a rather charming tale of an impressive gent called Zhuge Liang, who led his army across a particularly troublesome river. Not enamored of the suggestion that he sacrifice fifty of his men and throw their heads into the river as a rite of passage (funny, that), he decided instead to make something that replicated a head shape, and fooled everyone by coming up with a steamed bun or roll. Cunning. This ploy apparently ensured the army a safe crossing, and the term stuck.

Pork Belly Mantou

To make the mantou, mix the yeast with the warm water and a pinch or so of the sugar and set aside to activate. Once activated, mix with the remaining sugar and all the other ingredients in a large mixing bowl to form a smooth dough. Knead for about 10 minutes (this is much easier in an electric mixer with a dough hook attachment).

Shape the dough into a ball, place it in a clean oiled bowl, then cover with a clean dish towel and let rise in a warm place for about an hour or until doubled in size. Once risen, gently punch down (knock back) the dough and knead again for a few minutes, then return it to the bowl, cover, and let stand in a warm place for 20 minutes. Roll out the dough to form a long, thin rectangle that is roughly 28 x 6in (71 x 15cm)—don't fret, this is just approximate. Roll up the dough (from a long side) into a long log and then cut into about 10 small lengths, each about 3in (7.5cm) long.

Fill a saucepan with cold water for steaming. Line the steamer with cheesecloth (muslin) or wax (greaseproof) paper and place a few of the mantou on top (don't be tempted to add more than 3 or 4 as they will expand during steaming). Cover and steam for 20 minutes, then turn off the heat and let them steam for another 2 minutes. Do not remove the lid until the end of the cooking time. Remove the steamed mantou to a plate and repeat with the other mantou. Once they are all cooked, they can then be reheated in the steamer.

Meanwhile, to make the red cooked pork, place the pork belly in a saucepan, cover with cold water, and bring to a boil. Simmer for about 20 minutes, skimming off the scum that rises to the surface. Remove the

Makes about 10

INGREDIENTS
FOR THE MANTOU:

2 tsp active dry yeast

Scant 1¼ cups (275ml) warm water

1oz (30g) superfine (caster) sugar

4 cups (500g) all-purpose (plain) flour

½ tsp sea salt

1 tsp vegetable oil

FOR THE RED COOKED PORK:

1lb 2oz (500g) pork belly in one piece

1½ tbsp superfine (caster) sugar

2 tbsp vegetable oil

2 garlic cloves, peeled

1 thick slice fresh ginger, peeled

A piece of cassia bark (or a small cinnamon stick)

2 scallions (spring onions), cut into several pieces

2 star anise

1½ tbsp dark soy sauce

Scant ¼ cups (50ml) Chinese rice (cooking) wine (shaoxing rice wine)

1¼ cups (300ml) vegetable broth (stock) or water

Thinly sliced scallions (spring onions), to serve

pork from the pan and let cool. Discard the cooking water. When cool enough to handle, cut the pork into bite-sized chunks.

In a wok over a medium-high heat, melt the sugar with the vegetable oil. After a couple of minutes, once the sugar has begun to caramelize, add the pork (take care, it may spit) and stir to coat. Keep stir-frying this for about 5 minutes.

Add all the other ingredients to the wok and simmer, covered, for 45 minutes, stirring frequently. At the end of this time, remove the cover, remove, and discard the ginger slice, cassia bark, and star anise, then reduce the sauce until it is thick and glossy, coating the meat.

Reheat the steamed mantou in the steamer. Serve the red cooked pork in the split mantou, topped with some finely shredded scallions (spring onions).

Baked Bean Toastie

Ahh, the toastie—a student classic! Don't go getting all wistful just yet, you keen beans. Let's get the historical facts straight first...

In the 1970s, John O'Brien of The Breville Company invented his famous toasted sandwich maker, a device that clamps the crusts together while the sandwich is toasting, containing the filling within two pockets. The sandwich itself is now often referred to simply as "a Breville." There are many classic recipes, including cheese and tomato (many a chin burned by a red hot tomato slice slapping against it), and even canned spaghetti (who, me?). One I remember fondly from student days, however, is the baked bean toastie; dipped in ketchup, brown sauce, or steak sauce, this saw me through many a revision period, not to mention hangover. My friend once told me that his dad can get an egg to set perfectly in the middle of the toastie, so that the yolk was still runny when cut. Impressive, but I'm going to keep things simple here.

There is just one final thing to say about the toastie and that is a word of warning; never, ever underestimate the heat of that filling. The internationally recognized heat scale goes like this: 1) center of the sun; 2) inside of baked bean toastie; 3) other things that may be hot.

Makes 1

INGREDIENTS

2 slices white or brown bread

Butter, at room temperature

5½oz (150g) can baked beans

Grated cheese, such as Cheddar, Swiss, Provolone, or Monterey Jack (optional)

A dash of Worcestershire sauce (optional)

Ketchup, brown sauce, or steak sauce, to serve

Heat the sandwich toaster. Spread one side of both slices of bread with butter, and when the sandwich toaster is hot, place the first slice, butter-side down, onto the hot plate.

Empty the baked beans onto the bread and top with some grated cheese and Worcestershire sauce, if using. Top with the remaining slice of bread, butter-side up, and close the sandwich toaster.

Toast until golden and crisp. Serve with your preferred sauce.

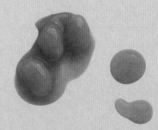

There are many variations on the breakfast butty, but my favorite is one I discovered at the famous Maria's Café in London's Borough Market. It's a classic combo of bacon and egg, but with a helping of bubble and squeak thrown in, all crisp on the outside and fluffy, cabbage-flecked potato within. The whole lot is crowned with a slice of melting cheese and served in a large floury roll. Add a squirt of your favorite sauce and this behemoth of a sandwich is guaranteed to blow your hangover out of the water. Then it's time for a snooze...

Makes 4

INGREDIENTS
FOR THE BUBBLE AND SQUEAK:

1lb 2oz (500g) potatoes

3½oz (100g) green (or Savoy) cabbage or other greens, roughly chopped

4 scallions (spring onions), finely chopped

1 tbsp whole-grain mustard

Sea salt and black pepper, to taste

Vegetable oil, for frying

8 slices smoked bacon

4 eggs

4 large floury rolls, split open

4 slices cheese, such as Cheddar or Swiss cheese

Brown sauce, ketchup, or steak sauce, to serve

Breakfast Bacon, Cheese, and Bubble Roll

To make the bubble and squeak, cook the potatoes in a pan of boiling salted water until tender, then drain and mash. Cook the cabbage in a separate pan of boiling salted water until just tender, then drain and mix well with the mashed potatoes, scallions (spring onions), and mustard. Taste, season well with salt and pepper, and then taste again. Cool slightly, then form into 4 burger-shaped patties.

Heat a little vegetable oil in a frying pan and fry the bubble and squeak patties until golden and crisp on each side. Don't worry if they break up; this just means more surface area and more of the good crispy bits.

Meanwhile, cook the bacon to your liking and fry the eggs. Lightly toast the rolls, then immediately add a slice of cheese to the top half of each roll to let it melt slightly. Put a layer of bubble and squeak on the bottom half of each roll, then top with the bacon and fried eggs and add a squirt of your sauce of choice (I favor brown, personally). Top with the cheese-topped roll halves (cheese-side down) and serve immediately.

Chip Butty

The chip butty is a sandwich that, for many people in the UK, is a real taste of childhood. Across Britain there are many names for the chip butty including chip batch, chip cob (East Midlands), or my favorite, "piece and chips" (Scotland).

A chip butty is often an added bonus element of a fish supper: white bread, thickly buttered, served with fish and chips. The diner stuffs said bread with chips, finishing with a blob of ketchup or gravy. Despite potential stylistic variation, there is one vital rule: the filling must always be "proper" chips, never French fries.

INGREDIENTS

Maris Piper or Russet potatoes

Vegetable oil, for deep-frying

Sea salt and malt vinegar, to taste

White rolls, split open, and sauce of your choice, to serve

Peel the potatoes and cut them lengthwise into slices that are about ½in (1cm) thick. Cut these slices into chips. Put the chips into a bowl of cold water and let soak for a couple of hours if possible. If time is short, rinse well under plenty of cold water. This process removes extra starch. Drain and pat the chips dry.

Pour some vegetable oil for deep-frying into a deep frying pan or an electric deep-fat fryer and heat to 350°F (180°C), then fry the chips until crisp and golden. Drain on paper towels.

Add salt and vinegar to the chips, then pile into the split rolls. Serve with a good squirt of your sauce of choice. Eat immediately.

Potato Chip Sandwich

For most people, the potato chip (crisp) sandwich was something discovered during school lunchtimes. A sandwich and a packet of potato chips in the lunchbox—WHY NOT COMBINE THE TWO?! The fragile genius of hungry juvenile minds.

There's nothing quite as satisfying as layering up those potato chips, then pressing down the sandwich and hearing that kerrrunch. This is the key to the success of the potato chip sandwich— the textures. That, and the saltiness.

The potato chips are used as a garnish to another type of sandwich filling or, for the hardcore, just on their own with butter. Flavorwise, I tend to go for a cheese and onion and salt and vinegar mash up, but of course, there are many possibilities.

Makes 1

INGREDIENTS

2 slices white bread

Butter, at room temperature, or mayonnaise

Optional fillings of your choice (e.g. ham, cheese, cucumber, pâté, etc)

Potato chips (crisps) of your choice

Spread 1 slice of bread with butter or mayo, then layer with your chosen fillings. Top with a layer of overlapping potato chips (crisps). Add the second slice of bread and press down firmly. KERRRUNCH.

While in the UK and US we might be found wolfing down burgers and kebabs after a night out, I like to imagine the Japanese scarfing down fried noodle sandwiches or "yakisoba pan" ("yakisoba" meaning fried noodles in sauce, and "pan" meaning bread). Apparently, this sandwich is widely available in convenience stores.

Noodles are fried with vegetables, such as carrot and bell pepper, then seasoned with yakisoba sauce (an intense, umami-rich concoction) and stuffed into a hot dog bun. The sandwich is finished with strips of pickled ginger, dried seaweed, and often sweetened mayo.

Makes 4

INGREDIENTS

Vegetable oil, for frying

4 slices bacon, cut into strips

1 green bell pepper

1 small carrot, cut into thin strips

½ small onion, thinly sliced

2 x 3oz (85g) packets instant egg noodles

2–3 tbsp yakisoba sauce (or make your own—see Cook's Tip below), plus extra for garnishing

4 white hot dog buns, split open

Strips of pickled ginger, to serve

Dried green seaweed (aonori), to serve (optional)

Yakisoba Pan

Heat a wok over a medium-high heat and add a little vegetable oil. Fry the bacon strips in this until starting to turn crisp, then remove from the wok and set aside.

Fry the vegetables in the same wok you used for the bacon, and when they are starting to color but still retain some crunch, remove and put to one side.

Meanwhile, cook the noodles according to the packet instructions, then drain.

Add a little more oil to the wok and add the drained noodles, stirring them around constantly. When they are beginning to get crisp in places, add the yakisoba sauce. Stir through the vegetables and bacon, making sure everything is piping hot.

When ready to serve, pile the noodle mixture into the buns and garnish with a final drizzle of yakisoba sauce, strips of pickled ginger, and a sprinkling of dried seaweed, if using.

COOK'S TIP:

Homemade yakisoba sauce:

3 tbsp oyster sauce

1 tsp dark soy sauce

1 tsp superfine (caster) sugar

1 tsp sesame oil

Sea salt, to taste

To make your own yakisoba sauce, simply mix everything together until combined.

The francesinha is a huge decadent beast of a sandwich from Portugal. It's layered with several kinds of meat, plus cheese before the whole thing is covered in a rich sauce made with BEER. Get in.

Thought to be a Portuguese version of the croque monsieur, it is said that a man named Daniel Da Silva, on returning from France to Portugal in the 1960s, tried to adapt the French classic to Portuguese tastes. The sauce is key here, with each family and restaurant having their own secret recipe. In fact, when researching this book, I sparked a very heated discussion between members of a Portuguese family; every one of them had strong feelings as to how it should be cooked...

This sandwich is not for the faint of heart, which makes it even more impressive that the Portuguese traditionally serve it surrounded by French fries.

Francesinha

Makes 2

INGREDIENTS

2 tbsp vegetable oil

½ onion, finely chopped

2 minute steaks (about 5½oz/150g each), sliced

1 linguiça sausage (Portuguese smoked sausage), sliced

1 cooking chorizo sausage, sliced

1 tsp superfine (caster) sugar

1 x 12fl oz (330ml) bottle beer (Super Bock if you want to be all authentic)

8oz (225g) can chopped tomatoes

A dash of hot chili sauce

Sea salt and black pepper, to taste

1 tsp cornstarch (cornflour)

4 slices sturdy white bread (something like sourdough will work well)

2 slices cooked ham

4 thin slices Swiss (Emmenthal) cheese

Heat the vegetable oil in a frying pan and gently soften the onion. Add the sliced steaks, linguiça sausage, and chorizo and cook until the pieces of sausage are starting to crisp and caramelize and the steak is cooked through. Carefully remove the meat and set aside. Into the pan with the onions, add the sugar, beer, tomatoes, and a dash of hot chili sauce. Simmer, uncovered, for 20–30 minutes or until beginning to thicken.

Meanwhile, preheat the oven to 400°F (200°C) Gas 6.

Taste the sauce, then season with salt and pepper. Mix the cornstarch (cornflour) with a splash of cold water, then stir into the sauce. Cook for a few minutes, stirring, until nice and thick. Remove from the heat.

Place 2 slices of the bread, side by side, in a baking pan (tin), then add a layer of the cooked steak, sausage, and chorizo mixture to each, followed by a slice of ham. Add the remaining slices of bread and then put the cheese slices on top. Pour the sauce over the entire sandwiches.

Bake in the oven for about 20 minutes, until the cheese is melted and the sauce is bubbling. Serve immediately.

The Luther Burger

Only in America? The Luther burger consists of a bacon cheeseburger, sandwiched between a glazed doughnut rather than a hamburger bun. Yes, you did read that correctly. It is apparently named after the singer Luther Vandross, who is rumored to have favored it as a snack, or possibly even invented it after running out of hamburger buns. There's no real evidence for this whatsoever but it's a fun story so I'm rolling with it.

A burger with a doughnut sounds unpleasant, but it's all about the combination of salty and sweet, which really works; think salted caramel, or bacon and maple syrup, for example. In fact, a more accessible version of this sandwich is just the crisp bacon inside the doughnut; the incarnation I would personally choose to eat. How brave are you?

Cook the hamburger to your liking in a hot pan or on a BBQ. Cook the bacon until crisp. Layer the burger, bacon, and cheese slice inside the doughnut. Serve and enjoy.

Makes 1

INGREDIENTS

1 hamburger

2 slices bacon (streaky)

1 slice processed cheese

1 plain glazed doughnut (the ring kind, not the round, filled kind), cut in half

COOK'S TIP:

The idea of the Luther may send your arteries running for cover, but think of all the ingredients individually...

Burgers = good
Melted cheese = really good
Bacon = excellent
Doughnuts = very good

Take a look at the following formula developed by Harvard scientists:

$$good + really\ good \times excellent^2 + very\ good = amazing$$

It clearly shows that this sandwich is going to be one of the best things you have ever eaten. And science doesn't lie. So don't knock this beauty until you've tried it.

Spamwich

Now we really reach the depths of the guilty pleasure pool with everyone's favorite chopped pork and ham in a can—SPAM. It's salty and it's fatty, which is why occasionally (very occasionally) it's so good. Other cultures embrace luncheon meat with much more enthusiasm than we do; the Chinese love it, although not as much as the Hawaiians, who even hold an annual festival in its honor: the Waikiki Spam Jam!

Makes 4

INGREDIENTS

12oz (340g) can Spam

8 slices white bread or 4 white rolls, split open

Lettuce, shredded

Tomatoes, sliced

Scallions (spring onions), sliced

Mayonnaise

Dash of hot chili sauce (optional)

Cut the Spam into ½in (1cm)-thick slices. Then it's just a case of layering everything up between the slices of bread (or rolls) to make 4 sandwiches. Serve as soon as they are made.

FOR SOME VARIATIONS ON THE BASIC SPAMWICH:

- Make it a breakfast Spamwich by frying Spam slices until crisp on both sides, then sandwich them in a roll with a fried egg.
- Gently fry Spam slices and serve between 2 slices of hot toast with a slice of melted cheese.
- Try using it in place of the Caramel Pork in the Banh Mi recipe on page 14. You'll have a Spam Mi!

Fish Stick Sandwich

So much of the appreciation for guilty pleasure foods seems to stem from childhood, and the fish stick (fish finger) sandwich is no exception. It's possible to make a very nice homemade posh version, of course, with tartar sauce and fresh fish goujons, but there is a lot to be said for the nostalgic joy of those orange-crumbed sticks, sitting side by side so neatly as they do.

Many a sandwich fanatic would favor ketchup in this situation, but I'm afraid that they are, sadly, mistaken. The only correct saucing is mayonnaise, malt vinegar, and plenty of salt and pepper. Sometimes I go crazy and use white pepper instead of black. A garnish of shredded iceberg lettuce provides crunch.

Makes 1

INGREDIENTS

Enough fish sticks (fish fingers) to cover the bread

2 slices white bread

Mayonnaise

Malt vinegar, sea salt, and pepper (white pepper is nice for this sandwich), to taste

Iceberg lettuce, shredded

Cook the fish sticks (fish fingers) according to the packet instructions. Spread 1 slice of bread liberally with mayo, then add the fish sticks.

Season them with vinegar, salt, and pepper, then top with the lettuce and the second slice of bread. Serve immediately.

Dutch krokets (croquettes) are log-shaped nuggets of meat ragu, covered in breadcrumbs and deep-fried. The construction of the kroket sandwich basically involves stuffing one or two of these deep-fried snacks into a soft roll or slice of white bread and saucing with spicy mustard.

The inclusion of kecap manis (sweetened soy) may seem odd, but Dutch cuisine has a heavy Indonesian influence. The Netherlands was once a colonial power, which considered Indonesia the most prized colony of all.

Broodje Kroket

Makes 4

INGREDIENTS

FOR THE BÉCHAMEL SAUCE:

2 tbsp (25g) butter

1oz (25g) all-purpose (plain) flour

Small grating of nutmeg

½ cup (125ml) hot milk

Sea salt and white pepper, to taste

FOR THE FILLING:

5½oz (150g) cold roast beef, chopped

½ small onion, very finely chopped

A small handful of button mushrooms, finely chopped

1 tsp kecap manis (sweetened soy sauce)

1 tbsp chopped fresh thyme leaves

FOR THE COATING:

All-purpose (plain) flour

1 egg, beaten

Milk

Fresh breadcrumbs

Vegetable oil, for deep-frying

Soft white rolls, split open, and spicy mustard, to serve

To make the béchamel sauce, melt the butter in a small, heavy-based saucepan. Add the flour, stirring constantly, to make a smooth paste, or roux. Keep stirring for several minutes. Grate the nutmeg into the milk, then gradually add it to the roux, stirring constantly. Bring this mixture gently to a boil, stirring, then simmer for about 5 minutes. Remove from the heat, season with salt and a little white pepper, and then let cool, covered with a piece of wax (greaseproof) paper, to stop it forming a skin.

To make the filling, put all the ingredients into a food processor and blend together until well combined. Mix with the cooled béchamel sauce and season with more salt and white pepper if necessary. Place the mixture in the refrigerator until it is well chilled (a couple of hours or so) and then form into 4 log shapes (krokets), each about 3in (7.5cm) long.

For the coating, cover a plate with some flour. In a separate wide dish, mix the beaten egg with a splash of milk. Cover another plate with breadcrumbs. Dip each kroket first in the flour, then in the beaten egg mixture, and finally in the breadcrumbs to coat all over.

Meanwhile, pour some vegetable oil for deep-frying into a deep frying pan or an electric deep-fat fryer and heat to 350°F (180°C). Deep-fry the krokets in 2 batches for about 5 minutes or so, turning occasionally, until golden brown all over. Drain on paper towels. The cooked krokets can be kept warm in a low oven while you cook the second batch.

Serve the warm krokets in soft white rolls with plenty of spicy mustard on the side.

Lobster Roll

The history of the lobster roll presents us with two options for making it, involving either warm cooked lobster soaked in melted butter (Connecticut-style) or cold cooked lobster mixed with mayonnaise (Maine-style). While I very much like the former option, I give a recipe here for the latter; when the mayo is kept to a minimum, it can be one of the most delicious sandwiches of all time. As lobster is expensive, it's also a serious treat.

Makes 1

INGREDIENTS

The meat from 1 cooked lobster

Mayonnaise

Lemon juice

Sea salt and black pepper, to taste

1 soft hot dog-style bun or 1 brioche roll (for uber-decadence), split open

A few finely snipped fresh chives, to garnish

Chop the lobster meat into similarly sized chunks and mix with just enough mayonnaise to bind, plus a very tentative squeeze of lemon juice (it's always possible to add more but impossible to take it away).

Season with salt and pepper, then load into the bun or roll and sprinkle with a few snipped chives.

Eat, feeling like the queen or king of the world, preferably with a glass of champagne.

There are seemingly infinite ways to make a cheese sandwich even more delicious, and dipping it in beaten egg and frying it just has to be one of them. "In carozza" means "in a carriage," which is surely a rather lovely way of saying that the bread is holding the cheese within.

Do not be tempted to use better-quality bread for this sandwich; it will be too robust and the mozzarella inside won't melt. It must be a cheap sliced white, no matter what the quality of the cheese inside. That's one hard life lesson right there, so just suck it up. One could, of course, go completely crazy and add a slice of prosciutto or Parma ham or a fresh basil leaf or two. Personally, I prefer the pure and simple approach.

Mozzarella in Carozza

Makes 1

INGREDIENTS

Sliced mozzarella cheese

2 slices cheap "plasticy" white bread

Sea salt and black pepper, to taste

All-purpose (plain) flour

Milk

1 egg, beaten

Olive oil, for frying (not extra virgin though, the flavor is too strong)

Lay the sliced mozzarella between the 2 slices of bread to make a sandwich, leaving a gap around the edges. Season with salt and pepper, then press the edges together so that they are pretty much sealed.

Cover a plate with some flour, then fill another wide dish with milk and a further wide dish with the beaten egg (add a splash of milk to make the egg go further if necessary).

Heat a frying pan, add some olive oil, then dip the whole sandwich (both sides) first in the milk, then in the flour, then finally in the beaten egg.

Put the sandwich straight into the hot pan and cook until it is crisp and a beautiful amber hue on both sides, and the mozzarella inside is melted. Serve at once.

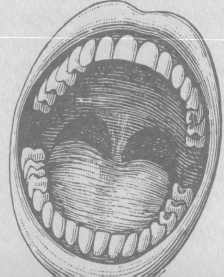

Lox and Cream Cheese Bagel

Historically, Jewish cuisine focuses on cheap and readily available ingredients; lox, which is cured salmon, was therefore a luxury item and is still expensive today. Lox specifically refers to salmon cured in a salt brine, and is different from the more familiar smoked salmon. Nowadays, however, the latter is more often than not substituted for the former, and that is what I suggest you do too, unless you are particularly keen to source it.

I retain the title of "lox and cream cheese bagel," however, as I felt it important to include a nod to the heritage of this Jewish classic. It is said that the ringed shape of the bagel represents the "circle of life," and the lox the saltiness of tears.

Makes 1

INGREDIENTS

1 plain white, poppy seed, or sesame seed bagel, cut in half

Cream cheese

Lox (smoked salmon) slices

A few capers, rinsed and patted dry, or slivers of red onion (optional)

Toast the bagel halves and let them cool slightly before spreading 1 half with cream cheese.

Lay the lox (smoked salmon) slices on top and then add the capers or red onion, should you wish to do so. Top with the other half of the bagel, and serve.

Croque Monsieur

The croque monsieur ("crisp mister") is a French classic; a toasted ham and cheese sandwich with a typically Gallic twist of decadence in the form of béchamel sauce. It appeared on Parisian café menus in 1910, although, as with many sandwiches, the original creator is unknown; some say that it was a happy accident—the result of workmen leaving their sandwiches too close to the radiator.

There are many variations on the classic croque, including the croque madame (with a fried egg on top); the croque provençal (with tomatoes and herbs); croque norvégien (salmon instead of ham); and croque Hawaiian (with a slice of pineapple), among others. A classic is a classic, however, so that's what you're getting here.

To make the béchamel sauce, heat the milk gently in a saucepan with the peppercorns, bay leaves, and onion. When it reaches simmering point, take it off the heat and strain into a bowl. Discard the flavorings.

Melt the butter in a separate saucepan, then mix in the flour, stirring vigorously to make a smooth paste, or roux. Start adding the milk slowly, mixing all the time. When about half of it is in, start adding it in larger quantities. The sauce should be smooth and glossy. Let it cook gently for about 5 minutes, stirring, then remove from the heat and season with salt and pepper.

Preheat the broiler (grill) to low.

To make the sandwiches, start by lightly toasting the bread slices. Spread with butter, then add a layer of ham, followed by a healthy layer of grated cheese to 2 of the slices. Add a second slice of toasted bread to each sandwich and top with a good blanket of the béchamel sauce. Add a little extra cheese on top, if you like.

Place the assembled sandwiches under the broiler and broil (grill) until the sandwiches are oozing, melting, and generally looking gorgeous. It's good to do this slowly in order to make sure that the cheese inside is melted too. When it's going nicely, turn up the broiler a bit to get the top all nice and bubbly. Serve immediately with some mustard.

Makes 2

INGREDIENTS

FOR THE BÉCHAMEL SAUCE:

Generous 1¾ cups (425ml) milk

A few black peppercorns

2 bay leaves

A slice of onion

3 tbsp (40g) butter

¾oz (20g) all-purpose (plain) flour

Sea salt and black pepper, to taste

FOR THE SANDWICHES:

4 slices sturdy white bread

Butter, at room temperature

4 slices cooked ham

Gruyère cheese, grated

Dijon mustard, to serve (you may also consider spreading some mustard inside the sandwich)

The Philly cheesesteak hails from—no prizes for guessing this one—Philadelphia. Brothers Pat and Harry Olivieri are generally credited with creating the base steak sandwich, which is thinly cut, quickly cooked, and then chopped even smaller while on the hot plate. The addition of cheese is said to have come later; the idea of one of their restaurant managers—Joe "cocky Joe" Lorenza. Cool name, no? And a cool idea, too; adding cheese generally is.

As we've discovered, rivalry is rife in the world of sandwiches, and the cheesesteak is no exception. Two restaurants, Pat's King of Steaks and Geno's Steaks are on opposite sides of the road and famously at loggerheads over their 'wiches. The main point of contention concerning cheesesteaks, in general, is whether they should be topped with Provolone, American cheese, or "Cheese Whiz." Provolone is, in my opinion, the most delicious and accessible, but knock yourself out and put anything you like on there, then claim one of your ancestors invented it.

Philly Cheesesteak

Makes 1 huge sandwich

INGREDIENTS
Vegetable oil, for frying
½ onion, sliced
½ green bell pepper, seeded and sliced
1 small garlic clove, crushed
Sea salt and black pepper, to taste
1 rib-eye steak (about 7oz/200g), thinly sliced
Provolone cheese, sliced
1 long, soft sub-style roll, split open

Heat a ridged griddle pan over a medium-high heat and add some vegetable oil. Fry the onion and bell pepper slices until starting to color, then add the garlic and some salt and pepper. Cook briefly, then push to one side of the pan or remove completely if the pan is small and the garlic is at risk of burning.

Add the steak slices and fry, breaking them up with a metal spatula until the pieces are almost cooked through. Season the meat with salt and pepper, then mix it together with the vegetables, top with cheese slices, and let them melt.

Spoon the meaty cheese mixture into the roll and devour.

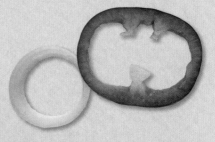

Club Sandwich

The club sandwich seems somewhat dated now, which is a shame. This club-house classic is said to have been the creation of a gentleman who came home late one evening with an appetite, to find his cooks retired to bed. What does one do in times of such hardship? Scour the kitchen for leftovers, that's what. He created the sandwich as a result of stuffing whatever he could find between two slices of toast. The sandwich was adopted by the club of which he was a member, and became known as the "club sandwich."

The sandwich started its life as a single decker. When it became a double is unclear, and although some say the extra layer is an unwelcome break with tradition, it has come to be one of the defining features of the modern club. I think it helps elevate the sandwich into the "luxe" category.

There are many possibilities in terms of variations, but the main players should include chicken, bacon, lettuce, tomato, and mayonnaise. Avocado, onion, and mustard are all nice too and sometimes (don't tell anyone) I add potato chips to create what I've dubbed "The Dirty Club." Think of it as an after-hours, by appointment only, variation.

Makes 1

INGREDIENTS

3 slices white bread

Mayonnaise

Dijon mustard (honey mustard would also be lovely)

Cold cooked chicken breast, sliced

Lettuce leaves

Sliced tomato

2 slices bacon, broiled (grilled) to your liking

½ avocado, peeled, pitted (stoned), and sliced very thinly

Toothpicks and pitted (stoned) olives, to serve

Toast the bread slices, then spread 2 slices with mayo and 1 with mustard. Add a layer of chicken on the slice of toasted bread spread with mustard, followed by some lettuce and tomato. Add a second slice of toasted bread and top with the bacon and avocado, followed by another layer of lettuce. Top with the final slice of toasted bread.

Cut into quarters and skewer each with a toothpick topped with an olive. Serve at once.

Pastrami on Rye

The refrigerator is a wonderfully useful kitchen appliance, but if it had existed since the dawn of time, we may never have invented other methods of preservation and would likely never have had something as fabulous as pastrami. Imagine!

Pastrami is traditionally produced by curing beef brisket in brine, which is then rubbed with wine vinegar and a selection of spices, including juniper, coriander, ginger, paprika, and pepper, among others. The meat is then dry-cured for one to two weeks before being smoked for around six hours, then steamed or braised. Phew! It's a lengthy process. Nowadays, briskets are more likely to be injected with brine, rather than soaked. Pastrami is also much softer than it once was, due to the invention of that handy refrigerator, meaning that a weaker salt solution can be used.

A man named Sussman Volk is credited with popularizing pastrami in America, although this is disputed (as ever) by Katz's deli, famous for their gigantic pastrami sandwiches to this day. The recipe below is for a classic pastrami sandwich; pile the meat as high as you dare. To turn the sandwich into a Rachel, which is a variation on The Reuben on page 16, add coleslaw and omit the mustard.

Spread 1 slice of bread with mustard and then layer up that pastrami. Top with the second slice of bread and see how far your jaw can open. Serve the dill pickles on the side.

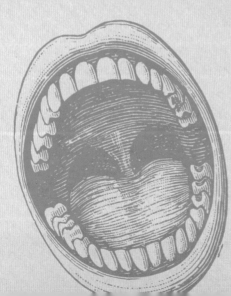

Makes 1

INGREDIENTS

2 slices light rye bread

Mustard, such as Dijon (although I prefer English)

Sliced pastrami, as much as you dare

Dill pickles (pickled gherkins), to serve

Confit Duck Sandwich

The luxe category would not be complete without some confit. The word "confit" means to preserve, specifically by rubbing the meat with salt, then cooking and storing it in its own fat. Aside from serving its purpose as a way of lengthening the shelf life of the meat, it is one of the most truly decadent cooking methods; the process intensifies the flavor and results in a silken texture to die for. Choose sturdy bread rolls for this sandwich that can hold their own against the juicy duck.

Makes 4

INGREDIENTS

1¾oz (50g) sea salt

3 garlic cloves, finely chopped

About 2 tsp fresh thyme leaves, picked from the stalks

4 duck legs (about 2¼lb/1kg total weight)

1lb 10oz (750g) duck fat

4 sturdy bread rolls, split open

Watercress

Mix the salt, garlic, and thyme leaves together. Place the duck legs in a non-reactive dish, then add the salt mixture and rub it well into the duck. Cover and refrigerate for 24–36 hours.

Preheat the oven to 225°F (110°C) Gas ¼.

Brush or wipe the excess salt mixture from the duck and pat dry with paper towels. Place the duck legs in a heavy casserole dish in which they will fit snugly in a single layer. Warm the duck fat gently until melted, then pour over the duck, covering it completely. Cover and cook in the oven for about 3 hours, until the meat is beginning to come away from the bone.

Remove from the oven, uncover, and let cool until the duck fat is cool enough to strain into a container. Strain it through cheesecloth (muslin) to remove any bits. The duck can now be served (see below) or stored in the container, submerged in the duck fat. It will need to be cooled completely, then kept in the refrigerator. It will keep for up to 1 month in the refrigerator (this recipe will make enough confit duck for about 4 rolls).

To assemble the sandwiches, shred the warm duck meat (discarding the bones) and pile it into the rolls while still warm. Add some watercress and serve.

Veal Schnitzel Sandwich

Schnitzel. Even just the word sounds a bit come hither and eat me: "You know I must be deep-fried." There are various versions of this meat-crumbed-and-fried filling around the world but my favorite is veal, which seems slightly more decadent than the rest.

Heat some vegetable oil for shallow-frying in a frying pan to a depth of 1¼in (3cm). Place the veal fillet between 2 pieces of plastic wrap (clingfilm) and use a rolling pin or meat mallet to flatten the fillet. Remove and discard the plastic wrap.

Cover a plate with flour seasoned with salt and pepper, then cover another plate with breadcrumbs. Put the beaten egg in a separate wide dish. Coat the veal fillet first in flour, then dip in the beaten egg mixture, then finally dip it in the breadcrumbs to coat all over.

Fry the crumbed fillet in the hot oil for about 4–5 minutes on each side, until golden brown and cooked through. Drain on paper towels and serve hot in the roll with mustard, a squeeze of lemon juice, and hot chili sauce.

Makes 1

INGREDIENTS

Vegetable oil, for frying

1 veal fillet (about 6oz/175g)

All-purpose (plain) flour

Sea salt and black pepper, to taste

Breadcrumbs, preferably panko breadcrumbs

1 egg, beaten with a splash of milk

1 soft white roll, split open

Mustard (such as spicy German or Dijon), a lemon wedge, and hot chili sauce, to serve

They really know how to make a good sandwich in New Orleans. Consider the Po Boy on page 66 and this, the muffaletta. Born in the French quarter, it is said that its invention can be attributed to the observant eye of a grocer, who noticed Sicilian workers buying all the constituent ingredients for their lunch and balancing the lot precariously on their weary knees while attempting to eat. The grocer suggested that they stuff everything into a sandwich for ease of transporting it into their mouths, and so the muffaletta was born.

Muffaletta

Makes 1 muffaletta for several people to share— serves about 4 (obviously the quantities here depend on the size of your loaf but, really, it's just a case of layering everything up inside the loaf)

INGREDIENTS

FOR THE OLIVE SALAD:

5½oz (150g) pitted (stoned) black olives

5½oz (150g) pitted (stoned) green olives

2¼oz (60g) Italian pickled vegetables (giardiniera), drained

1 tbsp capers, rinsed and patted dry

1 small red onion

4 canned anchovy fillets, drained

1 tsp dried oregano

Olive oil, for drizzling

Sea salt and black pepper, to taste

1 focaccia loaf (or a muffaletta if you're lucky or live in New Orleans)

10 slices capicola or salami

10 slices mortadella

10 slices cooked ham

8 slices Swiss cheese

8 slices Provolone cheese

To make the olive salad, finely chop the olives, pickled vegetables, capers, and red onion. Mash the anchovy fillets and add to the chopped vegetables, along with the oregano. Add enough olive oil to moisten the mixture, taste, and then season with salt and pepper.

To assemble the sandwich, cut the loaf in half and begin by removing some of the crumb from the inside of each half to make room for the filling. Brush the inside of the bread halves with a little of the oil from the olive salad, then layer up the meats and cheeses on the bottom half. Add a layer of olive salad on top, basically as much as you can fit in without it all falling out the sides, then cover with the top half of the loaf.

Press down the sandwich lightly, to secure everything but not squash it. Cut the sandwich into portions to serve. Serve any leftover olive salad on the side.

This meaty number hails from the Shaanxi province in China and is most commonly made with pork, although lamb and beef are substituted in Muslim areas. The meat is simmered in a mixture of aromatics like cassia bark, star anise, and ginger, then stuffed into a "mo" and garnished with fresh cilantro (coriander) and strips of pepper. English-style muffins are a good substitute for the traditional 'mo' and these are what I have used in this recipe.

Rou Jia Mo

Makes 5

INGREDIENTS

FOR THE FILLING:

1lb 2oz (500g) pork belly, without skin, diced

1 slice (about ¾in/2cm thick) fresh ginger, skin scraped off with a teaspoon

1 scallion (spring onion), cut into 3 large pieces

1 star anise

1 piece of cassia bark (or a small cinnamon stick)

1 tbsp Chinese rice (cooking) wine (shaoxing rice wine)

1 tbsp dark soy sauce

1 tbsp light soy sauce

1 tsp superfine (caster) sugar

5 English-style muffins

Strips of seeded green bell pepper

Fresh cilantro (coriander) leaves

Chili oil

To make the pork filling, put the pork into a pot, add all the other ingredients, and then add enough cold water to cover. Bring to a boil and then simmer gently, uncovered, for about 2 hours, topping up the water a little if necessary. The resulting sauce should coat the pork but not be watery. Remove and discard the ginger, star anise, and cassia bark before serving.

To serve, split and toast the muffins. Stuff some of the pork filling into the toasted muffins, along with some strips of green bell pepper, cilantro (coriander) leaves, and chili oil. Serve immediately.

Broodje Haring

I first came across the broodje haring or herring sandwich (or roll) at a famous street food stall in Amsterdam called Frens Heringshandel. One bite of the toothsome soused herring and I was hooked, lined, and sinkered; the fish has the most incredible buttery texture. The rich oiliness is offset by studs of sharp, raw onion and slices of sweet gherkin pickles or dill pickles, which also provide a contrasting crunch to the soft fish.

   This is one of the world's greatest fish sandwiches, but I leave you nonetheless with a piece of advice: either carry some breath mints or make sure everyone else within a 3-yard radius has eaten one too.

Makes as many as you have herrings

INGREDIENTS

Dutch soused herring fillets

Soft white hot dog-style buns, split open

Finely chopped onion

Slices of sweet gherkin pickles or dill pickles

Add 2 herring fillets to each bun. Sprinkle over some chopped onion and add slices of sweet gherkin pickles. Serve at once.

Bratwurst

The bratwurst is Germany's famous sausage; sizzling on many a strasse. "Brat" means "chopped meat" while "wurst" means "sausage." Some sources claim there are over fifty different varieties of wurst, varying in texture and flavor, depending on the region they come from. Some of the more famous bratwurst include the Coburger, which is traditionally grilled over pine cones; the Rote Wurst, a spicy pork variety; and the Würzburger Bratwurst, which contains wine and, frankly, has a name that is great fun to say out loud in a mock German accent.

Wursts may be broiled (grilled) or pan-fried, but one of the best ways to cook them is to simmer them in beer, before finishing on a hot BBQ grill or in a ridged griddle pan; this keeps the meat really juicy, ensures even cooking, and imparts flavor. It's hard to argue with a cooking method that involves beer in any case.

This is a no-brainer, really; broil, grill, or pan-fry your sausage, put it in a hot dog bun with hot German mustard, but never, ever, ketchup. Serve at once.

Makes 1

INGREDIENTS
1 bratwurst of your choice
1 hot dog bun, split open
Hot German mustard

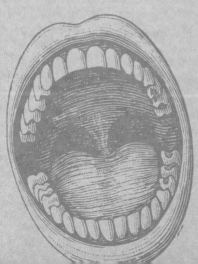

The word burrito means "little donkey," and the original burritos, from the North Mexican state of Chihuahua, were indeed small, containing only one or two fillings.

There is nothing little about the Mexican-American hulks we are familiar with today, however; huge lunking beasts capable of slaying a grown man at ten paces. These over-stuffed, aluminum foil-wrapped burritos we find in town are known as San Francisco or "Mission style" burritos. They typically contain numerous fillings such as meat, cheese, sour cream, refried beans, salsa, and guacamole.

This recipe makes a burrito that comes somewhere in the middle of the authentic and modern. It's like a little donkey that's become a bit fat.

Burrito

To make the salsa roja, toast the chilies in a dry pan over a low-medium heat for a few minutes, turning occasionally, then add the cumin and coriander seeds and toast until fragrant, moving the pan around to ensure they don't burn. Remove from the pan and set aside.

Preheat the broiler (grill) to high. Place the tomatoes, onion, and garlic cloves on the rack in a broiler (grill) pan and cook for about 15 minutes, until starting to char. Meanwhile, simmer the toasted chilies in a small saucepan of boiling water for about 15 minutes, until tender, then drain. Blend the chilies with the charred vegetables and garlic and toasted seeds in a food processor. Season the salsa with chopped cilantro (coriander), lime juice, sugar, and salt to taste. Set aside.

To make the guacamole, pound the chili to a paste with a little salt in a pestle and mortar. Halve, peel, and pit (stone) the avocados and add them too, bashing them up but leaving nice chunks in places. Add the juice of ½ lime and mix well. Stir in the onion and cilantro. Taste, and add more salt and lime juice if necessary. Set aside.

To make the burritos, wrap the corn tortillas in a damp clean dish towel, place in a dish, and warm through in a low oven—250°F (120°C/Gas ½)—for about 15 minutes. Meanwhile, heat some vegetable oil in a frying pan, add the onion and bell pepper, and cook until beginning to color. Add the steak pieces and fry for about 2 minutes or until cooked to your liking.

To assemble the burritos, lay the corn tortillas out flat and add the fillings in a horizontal line toward the lower half. Add a line of the steak mixture, followed by line of guacamole, and then one of salsa. Add a little sour cream, then roll the bottom side of the tortilla over the filling. Tuck in the sides of the tortilla and continue rolling until everything is contained. Serve the burritos immediately.

Makes 4

INGREDIENTS

FOR THE SALSA ROJA:

2 dried chipotle chilies

2 dried ancho chilies

1 tsp cumin seeds

1 tsp coriander seeds

6 ripe tomatoes, halved

1 onion, cut into wedges

2 garlic cloves, peeled

Chopped fresh cilantro (coriander)

Juice of 1 lime

Superfine (caster) sugar, to taste

Sea salt, to taste

FOR THE GUACAMOLE:

1 fresh red chili, finely chopped (seeded or not is up to you)

2 ripe avocados

Juice of 1 lime

½ small red onion, finely chopped

2 tbsp chopped fresh cilantro (coriander) leaves

FOR THE BURRITOS:

4 corn tortillas

Vegetable oil, for frying

1 onion, sliced

1 green bell pepper, seeded and sliced

12oz (350g) top sirloin (rump) steak, cut into small pieces

Sour cream

The man'oushe is a Lebanese flatbread, which is smeared with za'atar—a heady mixture of predominantly sesame seeds and thyme, among other ingredients (in fact, the word "za'atar" means "thyme" in Arabic). The still-warm flatbread is rolled up around various fillings: sprightly fresh herbs like mint and parsley, crunchy pickled turnips, studs of finely chopped onion, and creamy labneh (strained yogurt).

The man'oushe is often referred to as "Lebanese pizza," but here I'm busting out the artistic license and calling it a wrap, which makes it a sandwich (the same dirty trick can be pulled with lahmacun, or "Turkish pizza"—just wrap it around similar fillings).

Man'oushe

Makes 8–10

INGREDIENTS

FOR THE FLATBREAD:

4 cups (500g) all-purpose (plain) flour

7g sachet easy-blend dried yeast

1½ tsp sea salt

1 tsp superfine (caster) sugar

Generous 1 cup (250ml) warm water

1½ tbsp olive oil

Za'atar (available from Middle Eastern stores)

Olive oil

Fresh mint leaves, roughly chopped

Fresh flat-leaf parsley leaves, roughly chopped

Tomatoes, seeded and finely chopped

Red onion, finely chopped

Pickled turnips or other pickled vegetables, drained and sliced

Labneh or plain yogurt (it is easy to make your own labneh—see Cook's Tip opposite)

Ground sumac

To make the flatbread, combine the flour, yeast, salt, and sugar in a large mixing bowl. Gradually add the warm water, mixing until you have a soft dough. Knead for about 5 minutes on a lightly floured surface, gradually adding the olive oil as you do so.

Rub a bowl with a little oil and place the dough in it. Cover with a clean dish towel and let rise in a warm place for about 3 hours, until doubled in size. Once risen, gently punch down (knock back) the dough and knead again for a few minutes. Divide the dough into 8–10 pieces, then roll out into flatbreads, each about ¼in (5mm) thick. Cook the flatbreads, 1 or 2 at a time, in a hot, dry large skillet for about 3 minutes on each side, until brown spots appear in places. The cooked flatbreads can be kept warm in a low oven while you cook the remainder.

To assemble the sandwiches, mix some za'atar with a little olive oil to make it easier to spread and brush it onto each flatbread while still warm. Top with mint and parsley leaves, some chopped tomato and red onion, and some sliced pickles, then dollop with labneh. Sprinkle with sumac, wrap, and eat posthaste.

Makes 2

INGREDIENTS
FOR THE BURGERS:

1 small onion

½ green bell pepper, seeded

1 garlic clove, peeled

1 tbsp Worcestershire sauce

14oz (400g) ground beef (fresh beef mince)

Sea salt and black pepper, to taste

FOR THE SAUCE:

1 tbsp mayonnaise

2 tbsp ketchup

1 tbsp yellow (American-style) mustard

Pinch of dried oregano

Dash of hot chili sauce

FOR THE GARNISHES:

1 tbsp vegetable oil

¼ green (white) cabbage, shredded

1 onion, sliced

2 burger buns, cut in half, to serve

2 ripe tomato slices, to serve

Chimichurri

The chimichurri is a Dominican hamburger, and should not be confused with the Argentinian sauce of the same name, which is used in the Lomito on page 92. This "chimi," as the Dominicans call it, is basically a seasoned beef patty (or burger) served with fried onions and cabbage, tomato, and cocktail sauce.

The chimi has one very important accompaniment: ice-cold beer. The Dominicans appear to take their beer extremely seriously, which is more than all right by me. The glass should arrive at the table practically glacial and one should be worried about touching it with bare hands for fear they will stick and you won't be able to pick up your chimi.

To make the burgers, whizz the onion, bell pepper, garlic, and Worcestershire sauce together in a food processor until you have a paste. Mix this with the meat, and season with some salt and pepper. Shape the meat mixture into 2 patties or burgers. Heat a frying pan or ridged griddle pan and cook the burgers to your liking.

Meanwhile, to make the sauce, simply mix everything together and adjust the taste to your liking.

In the meantime, prepare the garnishes. Heat the vegetable oil in a frying pan and cook the cabbage until softened and beginning to color. Remove to a plate and keep hot. Do the same with the onion.

To assemble the sandwiches, toast the burger buns. Place a hot burger in each bun, top with a tomato slice, then some fried onions and cabbage, and finally drizzle with the sauce. Serve at once.

The Mexicans are just too good at making sandwiches. The cemita poblana is another example, this time from Puebla. It is crammed with meat fillings and topped with cheese (usually panela), plus avocado, onions, and salsa roja. The Mexicans have some glorious variations on this, such as pickled pig skin and head cheese. Go on, I dare you.

Cemita Poblana

Pour some vegetable oil for deep-frying into a deep frying pan or an electric deep-fat fryer and heat to 350°F (180°C).

Place the steak between 2 pieces of plastic wrap (clingfilm) and bash with a meat mallet or rolling pin until thin. Spread some flour, seasoned with salt and pepper, on a plate. Spread the breadcrumbs on another plate and place the beaten egg in a separate wide dish. Dip the steak in the flour, then in the beaten egg, and finally dip it in the breadcrumbs, to coat all over. Deep-fry the crumbed steak for about 8 minutes, turning occasionally, until golden on the outside and cooked through. Drain on paper towels.

Split the roll, remove some of the crumb from the top half and then toast. Stuff with the freshly fried beef, followed by some grated cheese, onion slices, and avocado slices. Top with a generous drizzle of salsa roja and serve.

Makes 1

INGREDIENTS

Vegetable oil, for deep-frying

1 thin-cut top sirloin (rump) steak (about 5½oz/150g)

All-purpose (plain) flour

Sea salt and black pepper, to taste

Fresh breadcrumbs, for coating the steak

1 egg, beaten

1 white roll, preferably topped with sesame seeds

Grated mozzarella cheese

Thin slices onion

½ avocado, peeled, pitted (stoned), and thinly sliced

Salsa Roja (see recipe on page 59)

Sabich

The sabich is a glorious Israeli sandwich, its history rooted in the tradition of the Shabbat breakfast of Israeli Jews. As no cooking is allowed on the Shabbat, some of the main fillings such as eggs and fried eggplants (aubergines) are cooked the day before.

Some claim that the sandwich was so named as it stems from the Arabic word for morning, "sabach," in reference to the Shabbat morning meal. Others claim it is named after the restaurateur who popularized it in Israel. Whatever the origins, it tastes magnificent.

The basic filling is adorned with a variety of garnishes, which may include Israeli salad (a chopped salad of cucumber and tomatoes), onions seasoned with sumac, hummus, tahini, skhug (hot sauce), and "amba" (a condiment containing pickled mango). Sounds good, huh?

Makes 2

INGREDIENTS

Vegetable oil, for frying

1 small eggplant (aubergine), sliced

2 cold hard-boiled eggs

½ cucumber, finely chopped

2 tomatoes, seeded and finely chopped

Sea salt and black pepper, to taste

Juice of ½–1 lemon

2 oval-shaped pita breads

Onion slices

Ground sumac

Tahini

Hummus

Hot chili sauce

Fresh flat-leaf parsley, roughly chopped

Heat a skillet and add some vegetable oil to a depth of ½in (1cm) for shallow-frying, then cook the eggplant (aubergine) slices in batches. Once cooked, set aside to drain on paper towels. Peel and slice the eggs.

Mix together the cucumber and tomatoes, season with salt and pepper, and then add a squeeze of lemon juice. Taste, and add more if necessary.

Warm the pita breads in a low oven or under a low broiler (grill), then split them and fill with the egg slices, eggplant slices, and some of the cucumber and tomato salad. Sprinkle the onion slices with sumac and add these to the sandwiches. Drizzle with tahini, then add a blob of hummus and a dash of hot chili sauce. Sprinkle with parsley and serve at once. Serve any leftover cucumber and tomato salad on the side, if you like.

The kookoo is an Iranian omelet, and the sabzi in "kookoo sabzi" means "herbs." Herbs are of great importance in Iranian cuisine, prized for both their flavor and health-giving properties.

The omelet is commonly wrapped in flatbread along with various garnishes. A dash of chili sauce is welcome here—as it is, let's face it, in many sandwiches.

Kookoo Sabzi Wrap

Beat the eggs together well in a bowl, then stir in some salt and pepper. Heat the vegetable oil in a frying pan or skillet and cook the herbs and scallions (spring onions) in the oil, stirring constantly. After a few minutes, add the beaten eggs. Turn the heat down fairly low and cook for about 10–15 minutes, without stirring, until set on the bottom.

Meanwhile, preheat the broiler (grill) to high.

Finish cooking the omelet under the broiler (but watch carefully, as it will burn easily). Slide out onto a plate and cut into sections to serve.

Pop each section of omelet into a warmed flatbread, along with some sliced pickled cucumbers and tomatoes, extra herb leaves, and hot chili sauce. Serve immediately.

Makes 1 large herby omelet; serves 4

INGREDIENTS

6 eggs

Sea salt and black pepper, to taste

2 tbsp vegetable oil

A large bunch of fresh flat-leaf parsley, leaves picked and chopped

A large bunch of fresh cilantro (coriander), leaves picked and chopped

A bunch of fresh dill, large stalks removed, chopped

6 scallions (spring onions), thinly sliced

4 warmed flatbreads (such as khobez), sliced pickled cucumbers, sliced tomatoes, extra fresh herb leaves, and hot chili sauce, to serve

Makes 2

INGREDIENTS

FOR THE MAYONNAISE:

2 egg yolks

About ¾ cup (180ml) oil—vegetable or peanut (groundnut) oil are both good, but don't use olive oil, certainly not extra virgin)

½ red onion, finely chopped

2 dill pickles, finely chopped, plus 1 tsp juice from the pickle jar

1 tsp yellow (American-style) mustard

Juice of ½–1 lemon

1 tbsp chopped fresh flat-leaf parsley

Sea salt and black pepper, to taste

FOR THE SHRIMP (PRAWNS):

Vegetable oil, for deep-frying

3 tbsp polenta or cornmeal

2 scant tbsp Cajun seasoning mix

12 raw jumbo shrimp (king prawns), peeled and de-veined

Beaten egg

2 white sub rolls or 2 x 6 in (15cm) lengths of baguette

Shredded lettuce—Boston lettuce or butter lettuce (Little Gem) or iceberg are good choices

Hot chili sauce

The po boy (or poor boy) sandwich is a Louisiana classic, consisting of fried seafood, most commonly oysters or shrimp (prawns). One of the defining characteristics is the bread, traditionally New Orleans-style French bread. It is claimed that no such loaf can be obtained outside the area, as the specific climate is what makes it so light and airy.

The history of the name po boy is debated, but a popular story is that it comes from the generosity of two former streetcar workers who served sandwiches to striking employees of their former company, whom they referred to as "poor boys."

This recipe is for a "dressed" shrimp po boy, meaning the seafood comes with a cocktail sauce-esque dressing, plus shredded lettuce and sliced tomato.

Po Boy

To make the mayonnaise, put the egg yolks in a clean bowl and whisk them together. Whisk in the oil, adding a few drops at a time and making sure each bit of oil is fully incorporated before adding the next. As you whisk in more oil and the mayo starts to thicken, you can start adding it in very slightly larger quantities until you are steadily adding it in a thin stream. Stop when the mayonnaise has reached the desired consistency. Add all the other ingredients, adjusting them to taste (for example, you may want a little more lemon juice or a little more salt). Set aside.

To prepare the shrimp (prawns), pour some vegetable oil for deep-frying into a deep frying pan or an electric deep-fat fryer and heat to 350°F (180°C). Cover a plate with a mixture of the polenta and Cajun seasoning. Dip each shrimp in the beaten egg, then in the seasoning mix. Deep-fry the shrimp for 2–4 minutes, depending on size, turning occasionally. (You can also shallow-fry them, but make sure you have 1in/2.5cm or so of oil in the pan and turn them over halfway through.) Drain on paper towels.

To assemble the sandwiches, split and toast the sub rolls, then load with shredded lettuce, the deep-fried shrimp, some mayo, and a dribble of hot chili sauce. DEVOUR!

COOK'S TIP:

Any leftover mayonnaise will keep in an airtight container in the refrigerator for up to 3 days.

The different types of kebab from various parts of the world are far too numerous to mention. Some of the best come from Turkey, and for me, this is the winner of them all— the adana kebab (Adana being a large city in Southern Turkey). It consists of highly spiced ground lamb mince, pressed into a flattened log shape and cooked over a mangal (Turkish grill/BBQ), which imparts an all-important smoke flavor to the meat.

Adana Kebab

Makes 4

INGREDIENTS

FOR THE KEBABS:

1 large onion, chopped

1 red bell pepper, seeded and chopped

2 fresh green chilies (seeded or not is up to you)

4 garlic cloves, peeled

1lb 2oz (500g) ground lamb mince—it is essential that the mixture is fatty; ask your butcher to add in some extra fat if possible

A handful of fresh flat-leaf parsley leaves, very finely chopped

Sea salt, to taste

1 green bell pepper, cut into chunks

Vegetable oil

3 tomatoes, cut into wedges

4 flatbreads, such as khobez or similar; pita breads are also fine to use

1 onion, sliced and seasoned with ground sumac

Plain yogurt

To make the kebabs, finely chop the onion, red bell pepper, chilies, and garlic. Mix this with the meat, along with the parsley and a generous amount of salt, and knead the mixture for 5 minutes. Shape the mixture into 4 logs and then flatten them so they're each about 2in (5cm) wide, then mold them around 4 metal skewers. Set aside in the refrigerator while the BBQ is heating, but bring to room temperature before cooking.

Light a BBQ for direct grilling and wait until the coals have turned white. Add the kebabs to the grill, avoiding putting them directly over the coals, and grill for about 7 minutes on each side, until nicely charred.

Toss the chunks of green bell pepper with a drizzle of vegetable oil, and thread onto skewers with the tomato wedges. Add these to the BBQ also and cook for about 15 minutes or until charred at the edges, turning occasionally. While the kebabs and vegetables are grilling, use the flatbreads to dab the kebabs, mopping up any fat that is melting from them and warming the flatbreads at the same time.

When cooked through, remove the kebabs from the grill. Holding a flatbread in the palm of your hand, place a kebab in the center. Close the flatbread around the kebab and remove the skewer. Open the flatbread out again to add some grilled vegetables, onion slices, and a drizzle of yogurt. Rewrap the flatbread. Repeat for the remaining kebabs.

Mint Chutney Sandwich

These spicy chutney sandwiches are Anglo-Indian picnic food: dainty triangles filled with a punchy blend of green chilies and fragrant herbs. The heat is tempered somewhat by the creamy butter, but some slices of crisp cucumber do so further and make a refreshing addition to the sandwich. Add them at the last minute to avoid the ultimate sandwich nemesis—sogginess. One must always consider structural integrity when in charge of sandwich-building.

Makes 1

INGREDIENTS
FOR THE CHUTNEY:

A large bunch of fresh mint, leaves picked

A small bunch of fresh cilantro (coriander), leaves picked

3 fresh green chilies (seeded or not is up to you)

1 garlic clove, peeled

1in (2.5cm) piece fresh ginger, peeled and chopped

1 tsp superfine (caster) sugar

Juice of ½ lime

Sea salt, to taste

2 slices white bread, crusts removed

Butter, at room temperature

Cucumber, thinly sliced (optional)

To make the chutney, put all the ingredients into a food processor with some salt and blend together until smooth. Add more salt, lime juice, or sugar, if needed. Transfer to a bowl and chill in the refrigerator until you are ready to make the sandwich.

To assemble the sandwich, spread 1 slice of bread with butter, then spread the other slice generously with chutney. Top with the cucumber, if using, then sandwich the 2 slices together, cut into triangles, and serve.

COOK'S TIP:

If you have any leftover chutney, it will keep in an airtight container in the refrigerator for up to 3 days.

Bosna

The bosna is Austria's answer to the hot dog. Very popular as a late-night snack, post-boozing, it consists of a couple of cooked bosnawurst (a pork and veal sausage flavored with citrus and marjoram), plus griddled onions and a curry-enhanced ketchup-based sauce.

Once the sausages are cooked, split a roll and place it directly where the sausages once sizzled; this means none of the fat that oozed from the wurst is wasted, and instead goes straight in your sandwich. Fat should be savored. Fat is flavor.

Mix the ketchup, mayonnaise, mustard, and curry powder together and set aside.

Grease a ridged griddle pan with vegetable oil and cook the sausages in the pan until cooked through and lightly charred on the outside. Toss the onion slices in a little vegetable oil and cook them alongside the sausages in the same pan.

Once the sausages and onions are cooked, remove them to a plate and keep hot. Split the roll and briefly toast it in the same pan, making sure to pick up all the lovely flavor that the sausages (and onion) have been so considerate to leave behind.

Stuff the sausages into the roll, topping with the onions and then the sauce. Scarf.

Makes 1

INGREDIENTS

1 tbsp ketchup

1 tsp mayonnaise

1 tsp German-style or English mustard

1 scant tsp curry powder

Vegetable oil, for frying

2 bosnawurst or other wurst-style sausages

1 small onion, sliced

1 large hot dog bun or similar-shaped bread roll capable of housing 2 wurst

A slight cheat, this one, as traditionally jerk wouldn't be eaten in a sandwich. It's such a summer classic, however, and it tastes so fine... basically, it's my book and I'll bend the rules if I want to.

The cornerstone flavors of jerk are allspice berries, Scotch bonnet chilies, and thyme. It must be cooked on a BBQ, preferably a "jerk drum," and there should be plenty of smoke. It's fun to soak some allspice berries in water and chuck them into the coals; this creates a beautifully scented smoke and a bit of food theater for guests if nothing else.

Jerk Chicken Sandwich with Pineapple Salsa

To make the marinade for the jerk chicken, put all the ingredients, except the chicken and soaked allspice berries, in a blender and whizz together until smooth. Smother the marinade over the chicken legs, rubbing it in well. Refrigerate for at least 4 hours, or overnight.

Allow the meat to come to room temperature and brush or wipe off most of the excess marinade before grilling the chicken on the BBQ. To set up your BBQ for the indirect cooking method, light the coals in the middle in a kind of volcano shape, then wait for the flames to disappear, leaving you with coals that have a light gray ash coating. Move them to the sides. This gets the indirect heat circulating around the kettle when you put the lid on. I find it helps to also brush the grate with a little oil. Chuck the soaked allspice berries into the coals before you start cooking, if using. The chicken pieces will probably take about 30 minutes to cook (although it depends on size)— always check that the juices run clear before serving.

While the chicken is cooking, make the pineapple salsa. Mix the honey with the juice of 1 lime in a bowl. Mix this with all the other ingredients in a larger bowl, plus some salt and pepper. Add more lime juice to taste, if necessary.

To serve, split the rolls, fill with the hot cooked chicken meat (discarding the bones), top with the salsa, and serve.

Makes 4

INGREDIENTS

FOR THE JERK CHICKEN:

1½ tbsp allspice berries, ground to a powder

¼ cup (55g) dark brown packed (muscovado) sugar

4 garlic cloves, peeled

1 tbsp fresh thyme leaves

A bunch of large scallions (spring onions)—about 5

½ tsp ground cinnamon

¼ tsp ground nutmeg

½ tsp ground ginger

½ tsp ground cloves

3 fresh Scotch bonnet chilies, seeded

Juice of 2 large limes

Slug of dark rum

1 tsp sea salt

Black pepper, to taste

4 chicken legs (or other chicken pieces of an equivalent size)

Extra allspice berries soaked in water (optional)

FOR THE PINEAPPLE SALSA:

1 tsp runny honey

Juice of 1–2 limes

1 small fresh pineapple, peeled, cored, and finely diced

1 small red onion, finely chopped

A small bunch of fresh cilantro (coriander), finely chopped

1 red bell pepper, seeded and finely chopped

4 white rolls, to serve

Kati Roll

Kati rolls originate from Kolkata, specifically a restaurant called Nizam, and they're traditionally a paratha (a flaky flatbread with paper-thin layers) rolled around various fillings. Today, the kati roll is made with a variety of Indian flatbreads, and the fillings are numerous, ranging from curried meats and vegetables to eggs and potatoes.

I've used aloo gobi (spiced cauliflower and potato), but you can use any leftover curry. In fact, I urge you to use up your leftover curry this way; we all know it tastes so much better the next morning too. Store-bought parathas are perfectly fine to use for this and in fact, are really rather good nowadays.

Makes 4

INGREDIENTS

FOR THE ALOO GOBI:

2 tbsp vegetable oil

1 heaped tsp mustard seeds

10 (fresh or dried) curry leaves

1 tsp cumin seeds

½ tsp ground turmeric

½ cauliflower, broken into small florets

3 large potatoes, cut into smallish cubes

Pinch of asafoetida (optional)

Sea salt and black pepper, to taste

Fresh cilantro (coriander) leaves

1 fresh red chili, thinly sliced (seeded or not is up to you)

4 parathas or other Indian flatbreads

¼ red onion, sliced

1 quantity Green Chutney (see page 22), mixed with 2 tbsp plain yogurt

To make the aloo gobi, heat the vegetable oil in a frying pan or skillet and add the mustard seeds, curry leaves, and cumin seeds. When the mustard seeds start to pop, add the turmeric, cauliflower, potatoes, and asafoetida, if using, and stir briefly.

Add enough water to just cover the vegetables and bring to a boil. Simmer, uncovered, for about 20 minutes, until the vegetables are cooked and the sauce is thickened. Season with salt and pepper, then add cilantro (coriander) leaves and chili slices, to taste.

To assemble each roll, heat a paratha in a dry frying pan or skillet for about 30 seconds on each side. Remove from the pan, add a line of aloo gobi, followed by some red onion slices and the yogurty green chutney. Roll up and serve.

The torta ahogada is a "drowned" sandwich from the Mexican state of Jalisco, particularly Guadalajara. Roast pork is stuffed into a bolillo roll, garnished with onions, and "drowned" in a fiery sauce packed with chile de árbol. Sandwiches come either "partially" or "well" drowned.

This sandwich must always be eaten with your hands, regardless of mess. To use a knife and fork is to cop out.

Torta Ahogada

To make the sauce, lightly toast the chilies in a dry frying pan until they become aromatic (do not allow them to char). Let cool slightly, remove the stalks and seeds, and then simmer the chilies in a saucepan of boiling water for about 15 minutes, until tender. Drain.

Make the sauce by putting the chilies and all the other ingredients, except the salt, into a blender, then whizz together until smooth. Add scant ⅓ cup (80ml) water, plus some salt, and blend again. Pour the sauce into a small saucepan and heat gently until warm.

Reheat the pork until hot, then split the roll and stuff the pork inside. Add some sliced onion. Pour some of the warm sauce all over the sandwich, garnish with a few more onion slices, and serve immediately.

Makes 1

INGREDIENTS
FOR THE SAUCE:

10 dried chiles de árbol

1 tsp sesame seeds

1 tbsp pumpkin seeds

Pinch of ground cumin

1 tsp dried oregano

Pinch of ground cloves

1 garlic clove, chopped

Scant ⅓ cup (80ml) cider vinegar

8oz (225g) can chopped tomatoes

Large pinch of superfine (caster) sugar

Sea salt, to taste

Leftover roast pork (with crackling if possible)

1 bolillo or other crusty sandwich roll, slightly stale (this makes it better for soaking up the sauce)

1 small onion, sliced

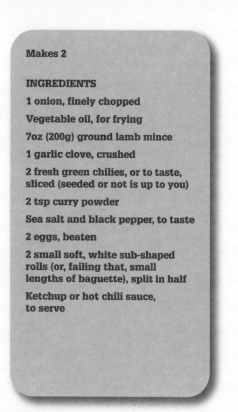

Makes 2

INGREDIENTS

1 onion, finely chopped

Vegetable oil, for frying

7oz (200g) ground lamb mince

1 garlic clove, crushed

2 fresh green chilies, or to taste,
sliced (seeded or not is up to you)

2 tsp curry powder

Sea salt and black pepper, to taste

2 eggs, beaten

2 small soft, white sub-shaped
rolls (or, failing that, small
lengths of baguette), split in half

Ketchup or hot chili sauce,
to serve

Roti John

The roti john is part of that marvelous group of sandwiches that requires the cook to scoop out some of the crumb to make way for more filling. It is essentially an omelet or scrambled egg sandwich, which is eaten in Singapore and Malaysia as a breakfast item but also generally as a snack.

Ground meat, eggs, and onions are mixed with chilies and curry powder, then smeared onto the halved roll before a deft hand flips the whole thing upside-down into a frying pan, rendering the eggy surface a gorgeous golden crust. The resulting roll halves (or lengths of baguette) can be eaten as they are or sandwiched on top of one another. Guess which method I favor...

Gently soften the onion in a little vegetable oil in a frying pan, then add the lamb, garlic, chilies, and curry powder. Cook, stirring, until the meat is browned and cooked through. Set the meat mixture aside in a bowl, leaving the frying pan on the heat. Add salt and pepper to the meat mixture, then stir in the eggs.

Press some of the meaty egg mixture onto the cut side of each roll half, then quickly flip each one, meat-side down, into the frying pan. Press down well and cook for a few minutes, until the meaty egg mixture is caramelized. Invert onto plates and zigzag some ketchup or hot chili sauce (or both) over the top. Serve at once.

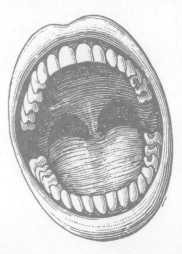

Deviled Ham Sandwich

Okay, so the idea of putting meat in a food processor may seem a little... wrong, but done right this creates a cracking sandwich filler, and ham is one of the best things to devil since, well, eggs, of course (to devil a food means to spike it with fiery condiments like mustard, or spice it with chili). Apparently it's possible to buy this in a can. Nothing good can possibly come of that—try this recipe instead.

Put the ham into a food processor with the mayonnaise, mustard, Tabasco sauce, Worcestershire sauce, red onion, and dill pickle. Pulse to a coarse paste (you don't want it too smooth). Taste, then season with salt and pepper if necessary (it may not need any at all).

Spread the paste onto 1 slice of bread, then top with another slice to make each sandwich. Serve.

Makes 5–10, depending on how thickly you spread the filling

INGREDIENTS

1lb (450g) cooked ham (proper stuff please, none of that processed rubbish)

4 tbsp mayonnaise, or enough to bind the ham

1 tbsp whole-grain mustard

Tabasco sauce, to taste

Dash of Worcestershire sauce

½ small red onion, chopped

1 small dill pickle, chopped

Sea salt and black pepper, to taste

Sliced white bread (2 slices per sandwich)

The souvlaki is a grilled pork kebab, which is a description that doesn't do it justice at all. Let's try again. The souvlaki is a skewer of succulent diced pork, marinated in a mixture of herbs, lemon, and olive oil, then barbecued until charred in places on the outside, yet juicy within. It is served in warm pita breads with sliced onions and tomatoes. The pitas should be toasted on the same grill as the meat was cooked on, to pick up the drippings.

Souvlaki Pita Bread

Makes 4

INGREDIENTS

FOR THE SOUVLAKI:

1lb 2oz (500g) pork leg, cut into 1in (2.5cm) cubes

2 garlic cloves, crushed

2 tsp dried oregano

1 tsp dried mint

Finely grated zest and juice of 1 unwaxed lemon

2 tbsp red wine

3 tbsp olive oil

Sea salt and black pepper, to taste

FOR THE TZATZIKI:

½ cucumber, peeled and seeded

Generous 1 cup (250ml) plain yogurt (full-fat, don't be shy)

Pinch of superfine (caster) sugar

½ tsp dried mint, or to taste

Squeeze of lemon juice

4 oval-shaped pita breads

Sliced tomatoes

Sliced onions

Fresh mint leaves

To make the souvlaki, mix the pork and all the other ingredients together in a bowl, then cover and let marinate for a few hours in the refrigerator.

To make the tzatziki, coarsely grate the cucumber into a colander and sprinkle with a little sea salt. Let stand for 20 minutes or so (over a bowl or the sink), then squeeze out as much water as possible. Mix the cucumber into the yogurt, then add some pepper, the sugar, dried mint, and a tentative squeeze of lemon juice. Taste, and add some more lemon juice or seasoning as you see fit.

When you are ready to cook the souvlaki, preheat a broiler (grill) to high or preheat a ridged griddle pan until hot, then thread the cubes of marinated meat onto metal or wooden skewers (if you use wooden ones, soak them in cold water for 30 minutes before use). Cook the souvlaki for about 10 minutes, turning fairly frequently, until cooked through and starting to char in places on the outside.

To serve, warm the pita breads in a low oven or under a low broiler (grill), then split and fill each one with souvlaki, tzatziki, tomato and onion slices, and fresh mint leaves. Serve at once.

The double comes from Trinidad and Tobago and consists of two pieces of fried bread ("bara"), enclosing a curried garbanzo bean (chickpea) filling. It is accessorized with a tamarind- or coconut-based chutney and a dollop of hot chili sauce. Originally served with a single bara, customers so frequently requested two, that the meal evolved into a "double."

Trini Double

Makes 12; serves 6

INGREDIENTS
FOR THE BARA:

1 tsp active dry yeast

Scant ⅓ cup (80ml) warm water

A pinch of superfine (caster) sugar

Generous 2 cups (270g) all-purpose (plain) flour

½ tsp sea salt

1 tsp curry powder

Vegetable oil, for deep-frying

FOR THE CURRIED GARBANZO BEANS (CHICKPEAS) OR "CURRIED CHANA":

1 tbsp cumin seeds

1 tbsp vegetable oil

1 small onion, sliced

2 garlic cloves, crushed

1 tsp curry powder

½ tsp ground turmeric

14oz (400g) can garbanzo beans (chickpeas)

2 potatoes, diced

1 fresh Scotch bonnet chili, left whole but pierced

Sea salt, to taste

A good handful of chopped fresh cilantro (coriander)

Tamarind chutney and Tabasco or hot chili sauce, to serve

To make the bara, mix the yeast with the warm water and sugar in a jug and set aside until the yeast is activated. In a mixing bowl, combine the flour, salt, and curry powder, then add the activated yeast mixture and mix to form a soft dough. Knead the dough for about 10 minutes (this is much easier in an electric mixer with a dough hook attachment). Place the dough in a clean oiled bowl, cover with a clean dish towel, and let rise in a warm place until doubled in size.

Meanwhile, to make the curried garbanzo beans (chickpeas), toast the cumin seeds in a dry frying pan over a low-medium heat until fragrant, moving them around the pan so they don't burn. Grind the toasted seeds to a powder with a pestle and mortar or spice grinder. Set aside. Heat the vegetable oil in the frying pan and soften the onion in the oil. Add the garlic and cook for a minute more, stirring, then add the ground spices and continue to cook for 30 seconds, stirring all the time until the mixture is quite dry.

Add the garbanzo beans, potatoes, and chili, plus enough water to cover. Bring to a boil, then reduce the heat and simmer, uncovered, for about 25 minutes, until the potatoes are cooked and the sauce is thick. Mash the mixture here and there to thicken even further, leaving plenty of pieces (and the chili) intact. Taste, then season with salt. Remove and discard the whole chili, then stir in the cilantro (coriander). Keep warm.

In the meantime, gently punch down (knock back) the risen bara dough, then divide the dough into 12 pieces and form each one into a thin, flat round shape, about 5in (13cm) in diameter. They should be quite thin.

Pour some vegetable oil for deep-frying into a deep frying pan or an electric deep-fat fryer and heat to 350°F (180°C). Deep-fry the bara in batches (cooking 2 at a time) for about 5 minutes, turning occasionally, until golden all over. Drain on paper towels. The cooked bara can be kept warm in a low oven while you cook the remainder.

To assemble each sandwich, take a bara and pile it with curried chana, add some tamarind chutney and Tabasco or hot chili sauce, and serve immediately while hot.

It's obvious that the picnic loaf came into being for ease of transportation. It can't be for ease of consumption, unless you have a mouth like a hippo. Regular sandwiches tend to fall apart or get squashed during transit; no such problems for the sturdy picnic loaf. The ingredients are layered up inside the loaf, meaning you get a lot more bang for your buck when it comes to fillings.

Picnic Loaf

Makes 1; serves 6

INGREDIENTS

2 zucchini (courgettes), sliced lengthwise

1 eggplant (aubergine), sliced lengthwise

1 red bell pepper, seeded and quartered

1 yellow bell pepper, seeded and quartered

1 garlic clove, crushed

Olive oil

Sea salt and black pepper, to taste

1 white cob loaf

A few tbsp black olive tapenade or basil pesto

Fresh basil leaves

10 slices salami

2 balls mozzarella cheese, drained, patted dry, and sliced

8 semi-dried (sun-blush) tomatoes, chopped

Mix all the vegetables with the crushed garlic and a slug of olive oil. Let marinate for about 30 minutes or longer if possible. After this time, season the vegetables with salt and pepper, then heat a ridged griddle pan and cook the vegetables in batches until soft and nicely charred in places. Set aside and let cool.

Cut off the top third of the loaf to make a lid. Hollow out the rest (bottom) of the loaf by pulling out most of the crumb from the inside with your hands. Leave a 1¼in (3cm) crust around the outside; it's important that this is a decent thickness so that it prevents the moisture from the vegetables turning the crust soggy. Reserve the crumb for another recipe.

Spread the inside of the loaf with the tapenade or pesto. Then, it's just a case of layering everything up inside. When the loaf is full, put the lid back on and wrap the whole thing tightly in plastic wrap (clingfilm). Weigh the loaf down by putting something heavy on top of it. Leave the loaf to press for a few hours at room temperature before serving, if possible.

To serve, remove and discard the plastic wrap, cut the loaf into wedges, and get that jaw ready.

Pulled Pork and Coleslaw Sandwich

Pulled pork is a BBQ classic, and a spectacular way to cook a pork shoulder. Long, slow cooking is fairly easy to achieve on a regular BBQ, provided it has a lid. The way to do this is to use indirect heat, which means sitting the joint on the opposite side of the grill to the hot coals and letting the heat circulate inside over a long period of time.

To make the pulled pork, the night before you want to cook the pork, mix all the ingredients for the rub together well using your hands. Liberally rub the meat all over with the rub mixture. Cover and refrigerate overnight.

The next day, remove the meat from the refrigerator about an hour before you want to cook it. Light the BBQ and when the coals are white, bank them to one side of the grill. Place the meat on the other side so that it is not sitting directly over any coals.

Cover and cook the meat for 4 hours. Each hour, add 8–12 more coals to the pile. This should keep the temperature fairly constant. The meat will be completely black on the outside after this time; don't worry. Remove the meat to a plate and start pulling it apart to reveal the meat within. Use 2 forks to shred it.

While the meat finishes cooking, make the coleslaw. If you can use a food processor to finely shred the vegetables, then do. I used a julienne peeler for the carrot and just thinly sliced the onion and cabbage by hand. Put the prepared vegetables into a large bowl. In another bowl, make the dressing by mixing together all the remaining ingredients. Mix this well with the vegetables. Season with salt and pepper.

Split and toast the rolls, then fill them generously with the hot pulled pork, drizzle with BBQ sauce, and top with a spoonful of coleslaw. Serve at once.

Makes enough for about 25 sandwiches (loads, basically)

INGREDIENTS

FOR THE PULLED PORK:

2 tbsp dried chipotle flakes or crushed red pepper flakes (chili flakes)

Pared zest of 1 orange, finely chopped

Scant 1 cup (200g) dark brown packed (muscovado) sugar

4 garlic cloves, crushed

½ tsp ground cloves

2 tsp ground allspice

1 tbsp sea salt

1 bone-in pork shoulder, weighing about 4½lb (2kg)

FOR THE COLESLAW:

1 carrot, coarsely grated, julienned, or shredded in a food processor

½ red onion, thinly sliced

¼ green (white) cabbage, very finely shredded

3 heaped tbsp sour cream

3 tbsp plain yogurt

1 tsp yellow (American-style) mustard

1 tbsp snipped fresh chives

2 tbsp juice from a jar of dill pickles

Sea salt and black pepper, to taste

White rolls (crusty white or even soft white rolls would work—it's up to you) and BBQ sauce of your choice, to serve

Balik Ekmek

The balik ekmek (literally meaning "fish sandwich") of Istanbul are legendary. The success of the sandwich rests entirely with the freshness of the fish, and the sandwiches are often cooked on and served from boats bobbing on the Bosphorus. I imagine the water twinkling in bright sunlight, on the grill; the hustle and bustle of cooking, and the babble of conversation as hungry customers await the latest catch.

    The grill-kissed mackerel is sprinkled with salt and crushed red pepper (chili) flakes, and the sandwich is garnished with salad and a charred green chili.

Makes 2

INGREDIENTS

2 fresh mackerel fillets (skin on), as perfectly fresh as possible

Olive oil

2 mild fresh green chilies, left whole

2 soft white rolls or 2 lengths of baguette, split open

Sea salt and crushed red pepper flakes (chili flakes), for sprinkling

Sliced onion

Sliced tomatoes

Lettuce leaves

2 lemon wedges, to serve

Light a BBQ for direct grilling (see also Cook's Tip). Once the flames have died down and the coals have turned white, it's ready for cooking.

Lightly brush the mackerel fillets with olive oil and cook them on the grill using a fish basket if you have one (a hinged metal cage for protecting fish on the BBQ—use the type suitable for cooking fillets rather than whole fish), turning once, until cooked and the flesh is opaque. This should take about 5 minutes (depending on size). Lightly oil and grill the green chilies at the same time.

Lightly toast the rolls on the grill, then fill with the mackerel. Sprinkle the fish with salt and crushed red pepper (chili) flakes, then add the salad ingredients and a grilled chili to each one. Serve at once with the lemon wedges.

COOK'S TIP:

Alternatively, you can cook the mackerel in a hot oiled ridged griddle pan. Cook the fillets, skin-side down, for about 3 minutes, then carefully turn them over and cook, flesh-side down, for about 2 minutes, until cooked and the flesh is opaque. Cook the oiled chilies alongside in the same pan and then toast the rolls in the pan.

The hamburger is now a symbol of America, but the history of the sandwich is unclear. It is thought to have evolved from the steak tartare, which found its way to Hamburg, ended up being cooked, and took the name of the city. This fledgling wasn't yet a fully grown hamburger, however, as the bun came later, when the patty reached America.

Three Americans claim the title of Hamburger Inventor. Louis Lassen of an establishment called "Louis' Lunch" claimed he invented it as a snack solution for a customer who was short of time; a classic sandwich story. The next contender is the modestly nicknamed "Hamburger Charlie Nagreen" who claimed he wedged a meatball into a bun thus creating the hamburger. The final claimants are The Menches Brothers, who said their great-grandfather and his brother invented it in New York. Hugely successful sandwich, multiple inventors coming forward. Surely you are not surprised by now.

BBQ Burger

Makes 4

INGREDIENTS

1lb 9oz (700g) top sirloin (rump) steak, minced, or ground beef of your choice; you want a good bit of fat in there basically

Sea salt and black pepper, to taste

4 cheese slices (processed cheese slices really do have a place here but, of course, use a cheese of your choice)

4 sesame seed burger buns, cut in half

Thinly sliced red onion

4 iceberg lettuce leaves, shredded

Sliced sweet gherkin pickles

Yellow (American-style) mustard

Ketchup

Heat a BBQ for direct grilling. Once the flames have died down and the coals are white, it's ready for cooking.

Divide the meat into 4 balls and flatten into patties or burgers. Do not add salt and pepper at this stage, as it will change the texture of the meat.

Once the grill is ready, season the outside of the burgers very generously with salt and pepper and add to the grill. Cook to your liking (about 4–5 minutes each side for a medium burger). Once you turn the burgers, add the cheese slices so that they melt slightly.

Lightly toast the buns for about 2 minutes on the BBQ and then add the burgers to the buns. Top the burgers with red onion, lettuce, sweet gherkin pickles, mustard, and ketchup. Serve at once.

5 WAYS TO BLING YOUR BURGER:

- Make it a chili burger: gently soften some chopped fresh green chilies in butter, then add a layer of them on top of the burger before covering with the cheese slice.
- Add 1–2 slices of cripsy bacon to your burger.
- Make a burger sauce by mixing together ketchup, mayonnaise, yellow (American-style) mustard, chopped Spanish onion, and chopped dill pickles. Season with a dash of hot chili sauce and Worcestershire sauce and add to the burger.
- Make it a "juicy Lucy" by stuffing the center of the patty with blue cheese before cooking (take care when eating; it's like cheesy lava on the inside).
- Top with mushrooms softened in butter with a crushed garlic clove, and add extra cheese for a garlic mushroom melt.

Caprese Panino

The caprese takes its name from the city of Capri in the Campania region of Italy. Most commonly eaten as a salad (insalata caprese), the ingredients of tomato, mozzarella cheese, and basil also work extremely well in panini. Each panino is made with a bread such as ciabatta or baguette, which is then stuffed and toasted in a special panini machine.

This is a sandwich exclusively for the summer, as a properly ripe tomato is essential. Don't even consider making it otherwise. I'M WATCHING YOU! Use the best-quality mozzarella cheese you can get your hands on too; the key to success here lies entirely with the quality of the ingredients.

Makes 1

INGREDIENTS

1 ciabatta roll or a length of baguette or other suitable long crusty bread

Olive oil

1 small ripe tomato, sliced

4 fresh basil leaves

Good-quality mozzarella cheese, sliced

Black pepper, to taste

Split the roll in half and brush the bottom half with olive oil, then layer on the tomato, basil leaves, and mozzarella. Season with black pepper, add the top half of the roll, and brush the outside with olive oil, which will make the top nice and crisp once toasted.

Heat a panini press and cook the sandwich until golden and the cheese is melted. If you do not have a panini press, use a hot ridged griddle pan and weigh the sandwich down with a heavy pan while toasting, flipping the sandwich halfway through cooking. Serve immediately.

Bulgogi Sandwich

Bulgogi, meaning "fire meat" in Korean, is a dish of grilled beef marinated in intense seasonings, such as soy sauce, sesame oil, garlic, and scallions (spring onions).

The is Korean BBQ at its best, and if you want to cook it outside, try threading the thin strips onto skewers to keep them under control; they can be pesky little blighters.

To make the bulgogi, place the steak slices in a sandwich bag or bowl with all the other ingredients, toss together to mix, then cover and refrigerate for a couple of hours.

Either thread the meat onto metal or wooden skewers (if you use wooden ones, soak them in cold water for 30 minutes before use) and cook on a hot BBQ over direct heat, or pan-fry the meat in a hot oiled frying pan or skillet until cooked through (discard the marinade). Do the same with the sliced green bell pepper.

To assemble the sandwiches, split the rolls and fill with the bulgogi, green bell pepper slices, scallion (spring onion) slices, and kimchi to taste. Serve immediately.

Makes 2

INGREDIENTS

FOR THE BULGOGI:

1lb (450g) sirloin steak, cut into very thin slices across the grain (it helps to chill the meat in the freezer as it's then possible to slice it more thinly)

4 tbsp dark soy sauce

1 tbsp sesame oil

1 tbsp sesame seeds, toasted

2 garlic cloves, crushed

1 tbsp superfine (caster) sugar

½ tsp crushed red pepper flakes (chili flakes)

2 scallions (spring onions), thinly sliced

½ onion, thinly sliced

1 green bell pepper, seeded and sliced

2 soft white rolls

1 scallion (spring onion), thinly sliced

Kimchi, to serve (kimchi is a dish of fermented cabbage, Chinese leaves, or other vegetables, flavored with ground Korean chili)

Lomito

INGREDIENTS

FOR THE CHIMICHURRI SAUCE:

4 garlic cloves, peeled

A large handful of fresh flat-leaf parsley leaves

A sprig of fresh oregano, leaves picked

1 shallot, peeled

2 tsp hot crushed red pepper flakes (hot chili flakes), or to taste

2 tbsp red wine vinegar

1 tbsp lime juice

Olive oil, to loosen

Sea salt, to taste

1 thin-cut sirloin steak (about 4½oz/125g)

Black pepper, to taste

1 egg

1 white roll

Mayonnaise

2 slices country-style ham

1 slice Swiss cheese

Shredded lettuce

Sliced tomato

Sliced onion

The lomito is a South American sandwich (found in Chile and Argentina), which is stuffed with steak or roast pork, plus other ingredients that may include, well, rather a lot actually—ham, fried egg, cheese, sliced tomato, lettuce, avocado, pickles, sauerkraut, mayo, and chimichurri sauce (an intense sauce made with vinegar, parsley, garlic, and chili, which bears no relation to the Chimichurri on page 62).

To make the chimichurri sauce, very finely chop the garlic, parsley, oregano, and shallot either by hand or by whizzing them together in a food processor. Mix in the crushed red pepper (chili) flakes, vinegar, and lime juice and loosen with olive oil to reach your desired consistency. Season with salt.

Heat a frying pan or skillet and add a splash of olive oil. Season the steak with salt and pepper and cook it briefly, turning once, until cooked to your liking. Remove the steak to a plate and let rest while you fry the egg in the same pan.

Split the roll in half, lightly toast it, then spread one half with mayonnaise. Layer on the steak, ham, cheese, fried egg, and salad ingredients, then drizzle very generously with chimichurri sauce and top with the other half of the roll. Serve at once.

COOK'S TIP:

Any leftover chimichurri sauce will keep in an airtight container or a sealed jar in the refrigerator for up to 2 weeks.

Ploughman's Sandwich

The traditional ploughman's lunch, famously served in British pubs, was always begging to be made into a sandwich; cheese, chutney, ham, pickles, apples, salad... and it all comes with bread? Duh.

There is only one way to make this sandwich even more enjoyable, and that is to eat it in a pub garden by a river, washed down with a pint of excellent beer, preferably served in a silver tankard with your name engraved on it.

Spread 1 slice of bread with mayonnaise and the other with pickle. Add slices of cheese and ham, and top with scallions (spring onions), apple slices, and lettuce leaves. Sandwich together and serve the pickled onions on the side.

Makes 1

INGREDIENTS

2 slices of your favorite bread

Mayonnaise

Sandwich pickle/relish (Branston pickle is a personal favorite)

Mature Cheddar cheese, sliced

Cold baked ham, sliced

Scallions (spring onions), thinly sliced

3 thin slices of apple (preferably a Pink Lady)

Boston (Butterhead) lettuce leaves

Pickled onions, to serve

Tomato Sandwich

The tomato sandwich is one of the simplest, which means that its success rests entirely upon the quality of its only filling—the tomato. A perfectly ripe tomato is often hard to come by, especially in colder climates, which is why when one is found, it should be consumed with proper appreciation.

A tomato sandwich should also be consumed instantly; everyone knows that if left to sit, the tomato can be the sandwich's worst enemy, and there is nothing worse than a tomato juice-induced patch of soggy bread.

Spread 1 slice of bread with butter. Add the tomato slices, sprinkle generously with salt and pepper, then top with the second slice of bread. Eat at once.

Makes 1

INGREDIENTS

2 slices white bread

Butter, at room temperature

1 perfectly ripe tomato, sliced

Sea salt and black pepper, to taste

Pan bagnat is a Niçoise specialty, comprising a hollowed-out loaf stuffed with hard-boiled eggs, salad, and a fishy mixture of tuna, all laced with silvery anchovies. A sharp mustardy vinaigrette is poured over the whole thing before it is wrapped and pressed.

This sandwich is perfect for a picnic therefore, as it can be left sitting around for hours and actually improve—quite a claim to fame in the sandwich world.

Makes 1 (serves 4)

INGREDIENTS

1 rustic, whole-wheat (wholemeal) round loaf

Olive oil

Fresh basil leaves

6½oz (185g) can good-quality tuna, drained

A small handful of capers, rinsed and patted dry

½ red onion, finely chopped

A small handful of fresh flat-leaf parsley, roughly chopped

Sea salt and black pepper, to taste

1 red bell pepper, seeded and thinly sliced

3½oz (100g) French beans (green beans), blanched for 2 minutes in boiling water, drained, refreshed under cold water, and patted dry

2 cold hard-boiled eggs, peeled and sliced

8 canned anchovy fillets, drained

A handful of Niçoise or kalamata olives, pitted (stoned) and sliced

Juice of ½ lemon

1 heaped tsp Dijon mustard

Pan Bagnat

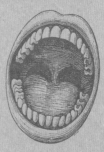

Cut off the top third of the loaf to make a lid. Hollow out some of the crumb from the rest (bottom) of the loaf, leaving a decent thickness of crust around the outside. Reserve the crumb for another recipe. Brush the inside of the loaf with olive oil, then add a layer of basil leaves to the bottom.

Flake the tuna into a bowl, then mix in the capers, red onion, parsley, and some salt and pepper. Add a layer of red bell pepper slices and green beans to the loaf, followed by the tuna mixture, then the eggs, anchovies, and olives.

In a small bowl, mix together the lemon juice with roughly double the amount of olive oil, the Dijon mustard, and some black pepper. Pour this all over the inside of the sandwich, then replace the lid of the loaf. Press down gently, then wrap the sandwich tightly in plastic wrap (clingfilm) and leave to sit for an hour or two at room temperature, or overnight in the refrigerator.

Remove and discard the plastic wrap, cut the loaf into wedges, and serve.

The hot brown is like cheese on toast, with a rocket up its backside. Created by Fred K. Schmidt at The Brown Hotel in Louisville, Kentucky, in 1926, it is an open sandwich packing some heavy weight, starting with "Texas Toast," which is bread cut to twice the thickness of regular bread, then buttered and broiled (grilled) on both sides. It is topped with sliced turkey, crisp bacon, and a velveteen blanket of Mornay sauce.

The Hot Brown

Makes 2

INGREDIENTS

FOR THE MORNAY SAUCE:

3 tbsp (40g) butter

⅓ cup (40g) all-purpose (plain) flour

Scant 2 cups (450ml) warmed milk—The Brown Hotel uses entirely heavy (double) cream here; do it if you dare

Sea salt and black pepper, to taste

1 cup (115g) grated Gruyère cheese, plus extra to garnish

FOR THE TEXAS TOAST:

Loaf of white bread

Butter, at room temperature

6 slices cold cooked turkey breast

4 slices broiled (grilled) bacon, kept hot

Pinch of paprika, to garnish

Finely chopped fresh flat-leaf parsley, to garnish

To make the Mornay sauce, melt the butter in a saucepan, then mix in the flour, stirring well to form a thick paste (or roux). Cook this over a fairly gentle heat for a couple of minutes, stirring constantly and taking care not to color the roux. Gradually whisk in the warmed milk and cook the sauce over a medium heat until it comes to a boil—about 3 minutes. Reduce the heat to a simmer and season with salt and pepper. Whisk in the grated cheese until melted. Remove from the heat.

Preheat the broiler (grill) to high.

Make the "Texas Toast" by cutting 4 slices from a loaf of white bread to twice the thickness of regular slices, then buttering both sides and broiling (grilling) each slice until crisp and golden on both sides.

To assemble the Hot Browns, place a slice of "Texas Toast" in each of 2 heatproof dishes. Top each with 3 slices of turkey breast and then pour some Mornay sauce over each. Sprinkle with extra cheese to garnish.

Put under the hot broiler until the cheese is melted and everything is bubbling.

Remove from the broiler and top each with 2 slices of hot crispy bacon, then sprinkle with the paprika and parsley. Cut the remaining 2 slices of toast into triangles and serve around the outside of the sandwiches.

The Elvis

Elvis Presley, "The King" of rock 'n' roll, surely needs no introduction. He was renowned for loving his high-calorie snacks, especially when cooked by his mother. Aww. This, apparently, was his favorite sandwich: a sweet and salty combination of peanut butter, banana, and sizzling streaky bacon. Elvis clearly wasn't a man to do things by halves, however, so the sandwich, once built, was reputedly fried in butter. It can be served with or without a drizzle of honey.

Preheat the broiler (grill) to high. Broil (grill) the bacon until crisp. Spread 1 slice of bread with peanut butter, then top with the banana slices and bacon, followed by the second slice of bread.

Melt a generous knob of butter in a frying pan or skillet and cook the sandwich until golden and crisp on both sides. Serve at once with a drizzle of honey, if you like.

Makes 1

INGREDIENTS

3 slices streaky bacon

2 slices white bread

Smooth peanut butter (or crunchy if you prefer)

1 banana, sliced

Butter, for frying

A drizzle of honey, to serve (optional)

Bauru's Sandwich

Bauru's sandwich is connected to both a person and a place. The person is not famous, however, and there are many sandwiches that are connected with cities around the world. What makes this sandwich special is the way that the city of Bauru in São Paulo has embraced it, to the extent that it is named as the city's official sandwich, the recipe is set out in municipal law, and there is an official certification program in place to protect it. Now those are the benefits of being well connected.

Incidentally, the sandwich was originally named after a student who was nicknamed after the city (real name Casimiro Pinto Neto), who, in 1934, asked for this specific sandwich in his local student eatery, Ponto Chic. "Bauru's sandwich" fast became the most popular item on the menu.

Makes 1

INGREDIENTS

1 French-style crusty white roll, short length of baguette, or Portuguese-style roll

4 slices cold roast beef

1 tomato, sliced

1 dill pickle, sliced

4 slices mozzarella cheese

Preheat the oven to 325°F (170°C) Gas 3.

Split the roll and remove most of the crumb inside. Layer on the roast beef, tomato, dill pickle, and mozzarella cheese.

Place on a baking sheet and bake in the oven for about 10 minutes, until the cheese is melted. Serve immediately.

Paddington Bear's Marmalade Sandwich

The adorable and ever polite bear from darkest Peru is famous for both his strong look (duffel coat, hat, accessorized with briefcase—he worked it) and his love of marmalade sandwiches. He loved those sandwiches so much in fact, that he kept one under his hat "in case of emergencies."

Makes 1

INGREDIENTS

2 slices bread

Marmalade

Bit of a no-brainer this one…

Simply assemble the sandwich using the bread and marmalade of your choice, then devour.

The Schumwich

The favorite lunch of New York's senior senator, Chuck Schumer, is packing (deep breath) roast beef, banana peppers (banana chilies), jalapeños, onions, tomatoes, double pickles, mayo, and mustard on Italian bread. I can only but imagine the pickle-laced onion breath.

   Schumer has reportedly thrown a tantrum should he feel insufficient attention has been paid to the making of his sandwich, berating aides who failed to watch every layer of construction with an eagle eye.

Spread one half of the roll with mayonnaise and the other with mustard. Fill the roll by layering on the roast beef, followed by the tomato, banana peppers (banana chilies), red onion, dill pickles, and pickled jalapeño slices. Season with salt and pepper and serve.

Makes 1

INGREDIENTS

1 Italian-style crusty white roll, split open

Mayonnaise

Yellow (American-style) mustard

3 slices cold roast beef

1 tomato, sliced

Sliced (seeded) banana peppers (banana chilies), mild green Turkish peppers, or yellow bell peppers

Sliced red onion

Sliced dill pickles—as many as you dare

Pickled jalapeño slices

Sea salt and black pepper, to taste

Ramon Barros Luco was president of Chile in the early 1900s. This was his favorite sandwich, which, unsurprisingly, is how it ended up being named after him. It's a simple affair to be honest, a combination of steak and melted cheese. It's not going to win any prizes for creativity, but is pretty damn tasty nonetheless.

Barros Luco

Heat a greased frying pan or skillet until hot. Season the steak with salt and pepper, then cook it to your liking in the hot pan.

Split the roll in half and rub the cut sides with the cut garlic clove. Add the steak to the sandwich and dust with cumin, top with red chili, and, finally, the cheese.

Toast the sandwich in a sandwich toaster or in a greased frying pan or skillet, until golden all over. Serve immediately.

Makes 1

INGREDIENTS

1 small thin-cut sirloin steak (about 4½oz/125g)

Sea salt and black pepper, to taste

1 white roll

1 garlic clove, peeled and cut in half

Ground cumin, for dusting

1 fresh red chili, finely chopped (seeded or not is up to you)

Sliced cheese, for melting (Swiss cheese would work well here)

The Gatsby

The Gatsby is named after Jay Gatsby, the extravagant millionaire protagonist in F. Scott Fitzgerald's 1925 novel "The Great Gatsby." The sandwich was not named so by its creator however (a man called Rashaad Pandy of "Super Fisheries"), but rather by one of his customers, who upon eating it exclaimed, "This is fantastic—a Gatsby smash!"—the comment is explained by the fact that the movie had recently been screened nearby with great success. Pandy had created it on a whim, having run out of all other ingredients.

The Gatsby consists of a soft, sub-style roll with various fillings, including meat such as masala steak or bologna, the wonderfully named "slap chips" (French fries doused in vinegar), and a condiment, such as piri piri sauce or Indian achar (a pickle). Although the meat and sauces may vary, it is the French fries that make this sandwich a "Gatsby."

Repeat after me: we must always pay respect when double carbs are involved... we must always pay respect when double carbs are involved...

In a hot frying pan or skillet, quickly cook the mortadella slices on both sides until crisp.

Douse the French fries in vinegar and salt. Layer the mortadella, French fries, and lettuce in the roll and top with piri piri sauce. Serve immediately.

Makes 1

INGREDIENTS
Mortadella slices
Hot French fries
Malt vinegar
Sea salt, to taste
Shredded iceberg lettuce
1 soft sub-style roll, split open
Piri piri sauce

Poor old coronation chicken; it started its life with such high status and aspirations, invented, as it was, to celebrate the coronation of Queen Elizabeth II in 1953. It is often claimed that the dish was created by celebrity florist Constance Spry, but credit must really go to her lesser-known business partner Rosemary Hume, founder of the Le Cordon Bleu Cookery School. Let's pay it where it's due.

A mixture of cold chicken, mayonnaise, and curry powder (individual spices were rarely available in post-war Britain), the dish was pitched as the perfect mixture of exotic convenience.

What was once one of the UK's most popular sandwich fillings is sadly now more familiar as a washed-out service station staple; a terrible shame, because the idea of lightly currying meat is lovely. When approached with a careful hand, coronation chicken can be subtly fragrant and delicious.

Coronation Chicken

Makes 2

INGREDIENTS

½ small onion, finely chopped

1 tbsp vegetable oil

½ tbsp good-quality curry powder

3 tbsp mayonnaise

3 tbsp plain yogurt

1 tbsp mango chutney

9oz (250g) leftover cold roast chicken meat, chopped

A small handful of fresh cilantro (coriander) leaves, chopped

A small handful of toasted slivered (flaked) almonds (optional)

Juice of ½ lime, or to taste

Sea salt and black pepper, to taste

4 slices soft white bread

In a small frying pan or skillet, gently cook the onion in the vegetable oil, until it starts to color. Add the curry powder and cook for 2 minutes, stirring all the time to prevent burning. Remove from the heat and let cool.

Mix together the mayonnaise and yogurt, then stir in the mango chutney. When the onion mixture is cool, add that too. Mix this sauce with the chicken meat. Stir in the cilantro (coriander) and toasted almonds, if using. Add a little lime juice (you can always add more) and salt and pepper, to taste.

Spread 2 slices of bread with the chicken mixture, then top with the remaining 2 slices of bread. Cut the sandwiches into triangles, fingers, or squares, and serve.

The Dagwood is surely a contender for one of the most outrageous sandwiches of all time and should be assembled with caution by a fully consenting adult. It is named after Dagwood Bumstead, a character in the comic strip "Blondie," who was known for constructing skyscrapers with multiple layers of bread, meats, cheese, and garnishes. Apparently his kitchen capabilities stretched only to layering up the various leftovers foraged from his refrigerator.

It's really just a case of throwing caution to the wind and piling up your favorite ingredients. The sandwich is then skewered with a long stick topped with two stuffed green olives. You may need a few friends to help you eat it. If you don't, then you have my full admiration.

The Dagwood

Lay out the 4 slices of bread and spread 2 with mustard and 2 with mayo. Then it's just a case of layering everything up. Start with a slice of Swiss cheese on 1 slice of bread, then maybe some ham, a slice of tomato, a dill pickle, and some scallion (spring onion), before adding the next slice of bread and then continuing with all the remaining fillings and the remaining bread slices, until your beautiful monster has been perfected.

Skewer the whole thing right down through the middle, and crown the skewer with the 2 stuffed olives.

Take a deep breath, and do what you have to do.

Makes 1

INGREDIENTS

4 slices light rye bread

Yellow (American-style) mustard

Mayonnaise

2 slices Swiss cheese

4 slices cooked ham

3 slices tomato

2 dill pickles, sliced lengthwise

1 scallion (spring onion), thinly sliced

2 slices smoked or regular Cheddar cheese (or use sharp Provolone or Monterey Jack, if you prefer)

4 slices salami

3 slices pastrami

1 cold cooked chicken breast, sliced

Iceberg lettuce, shredded

A long wooden or metal skewer and 2 stuffed green olives, to garnish

Queen Alexandra's Sandwich

In 1863, Alexandra of Denmark married the British Edward VII and became Queen of Great Britain. Result. She is said to have had a soft spot for these intensely savory sandwiches consisting of poached chicken, boiled tongue, and a mustard-laced butter. It is essential to remove the crusts before serving; these sandwiches need to be dainty enough for a queen. If you're feeling generous, give the leftover crusts to the poor.

Makes 2

INGREDIENTS

FOR THE MUSTARD BUTTER:

2 tbsp (25g) butter, at room temperature

1 tsp Dijon mustard, or to taste

A squeeze of lemon juice

1 cold cooked (ideally poached) chicken breast

Mayonnaise, to bind

A dash of hot chili sauce

Sea salt and black pepper, to taste

4 slices thinly cut white bread

2 slices cold boiled tongue or cold roast lamb

A small handful of salad cress

To make the mustard butter, combine the butter, mustard, and lemon juice to make a smooth paste.

Cut the chicken breast into small chunks and place in a bowl with some mayonnaise to bind—use as much as you like. Add a dash of hot chili sauce and season with salt and pepper.

To assemble the sandwiches, spread 2 slices of bread with the mustard butter. Lay a slice of tongue or roast lamb on each, then add the chicken mixture. Finish with a sprinkle of salad cress and add the top slices of bread.

Remove the crusts and cut into dainty squares or triangles as you see fit for a queen. Serve at once.

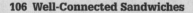

Shooter's Sandwich

This sandwich is basically a portable version of a beef Wellington; what's not to like about that? This hollowed-out loaf, stuffed with steak, onion, and mushrooms was apparently invented as sustenance for the Edwardian gentleman while out shooting. It could be made the night before and pressed, then sliced into wedges and packed off with the hunt the next morning. This is simple to make; patience is the most difficult ingredient to master.

Makes 1; Serves 6

INGREDIENTS

FOR THE DUXELLES::

2 tbsp (25g) butter

8 shallots, very finely chopped

14oz (400g) button or chestnut mushrooms, finely chopped

A sprig of fresh thyme, leaves picked

2 garlic cloves, crushed

A splash of brandy

Sea salt and black pepper, to taste

2 steaks, such as rib-eye or sirloin, which will fill the loaf (the size of each steak will depend on the size of loaf used)

1 large round white cob loaf

Horseradish sauce

Dijon mustard

First, make the duxelles by melting the butter in a frying pan or skillet and cooking the shallots and mushrooms slowly until almost all the moisture is gone. Add the thyme, garlic, and brandy and cook again until reduced and nearly all the brandy has cooked off. Season with salt and pepper. Remove from the heat and set aside.

Cook the steaks by heating a ridged griddle pan until screaming hot, then season the steaks heavily with salt and pepper just before putting them into the pan. Cook until medium-rare.

Cut off the top third of the loaf to make a lid, then hollow out the rest, reserving the crumb for use in another recipe. Spread some horseradish sauce on the bottom of the loaf, then add the first steak, followed by the duxelles. Add the second steak. Don't worry if it pokes out of the top, as the sandwich will be pressed overnight. Spread Dijon mustard on the cut side of the lid, then put the lid back on the loaf.

Wrap the sandwich in wax (greaseproof) paper and tie it up with string. Do this tightly. Wrap the whole thing in aluminum foil, then put it in the refrigerator where it can rest overnight. Weigh the top of the sandwich down with something good and heavy. This may require several heavy pans or whatever you have at your disposal. Just make sure it's properly pressed.

The next day, remove the weights and remove and discard the wrappings, then cut the loaf into wedges and serve.

Meatball Sub

"Subs" are not known so much in the UK apart from in relation to that strange-smelling sandwich bar with a presence on every high street (what IS that smell?). In the US, however, they're very popular and also go by the name of hoagies, grinders (don't ever Google "meatball grinder"—just trust me), torpedoes, or heroes. The name refers to the style of roll used, which is an elongated shape, and the name varies depending on which part of the country you find yourself in.

To make the meatballs, put the bread in a small bowl and cover with the milk, allowing it to soak in, then mash to a paste with a fork. Mix the paste with all the other meatball ingredients, except the flour and vegetable oil. Shape the mixture into large walnut-sized meatballs, then chill them in the refrigerator for at least 30 minutes.

When you are ready to cook the meatballs, cover a plate with flour, then roll each meatball around in it to cover completely. Cook the meatballs in some vegetable oil in a frying pan or skillet for about 5 minutes, until browned all over, then set aside to drain on paper towels, while you prepare the sauce. The meatballs don't need to be cooked fully, as they will be simmered in the sauce later.

To make the sauce, heat the vegetable oil in a frying pan or skillet and gently cook the garlic and crushed red pepper (chili) flakes until the garlic just begins to color. Add the wine and let it bubble up for a minute or so. Add the tomatoes, sugar, bay leaf, water or broth (stock), and some salt and pepper. Bring to a boil, then add the meatballs. Let the mixture simmer, uncovered, for 30–40 minutes, until the sauce is rich and thick and the meatballs are cooked. Stir in the basil.

Meanwhile, cook the roasted vegetables. Preheat the oven to 400°F (200°C) Gas 6.

Cut the bell pepper and onion into wedges, place in a roasting pan, season with salt and pepper, and drizzle with some olive oil. Mix well. Roast in the oven for about 30 minutes, until soft and charred in places.

Preheat the broiler (grill) to high.

To serve, split the subs, then scoop out some of the crumb from the bottom half of each one so you can fit the meatballs in more easily. Lightly toast the bottom halves of the subs. Top each one with some of the meatballs and sauce, then some cheese slices, and place under the broiler so that the cheese melts. Toast the top halves of the rolls also. Top the cheesy meatballs with the roasted veg, then add the top half of each sub. Serve at once.

Make sure you do some serious exercise the next day…

Makes 4

INGREDIENTS

FOR THE MEATBALLS:

1 thick slice white bread, crusts removed

A few tbsp milk

9oz (250g) ground pork mince

9oz (250g) ground beef mince

2 tbsp finely chopped fresh flat-leaf parsley

4 tbsp finely grated fresh Parmesan cheese

1 small onion, very finely chopped

Sea salt and black pepper, to taste

All-purpose (plain) flour, for dusting

Vegetable oil, for frying

FOR THE SAUCE:

2 tbsp vegetable oil

4 garlic cloves, finely chopped

Good pinch of crushed red pepper flakes (chili flakes)

A splash of red wine

14oz (400g) can chopped tomatoes

Pinch of superfine (caster) sugar

1 bay leaf, torn

A splash of water or beef or vegetable broth (stock)

A small bunch of fresh basil, shredded

FOR THE ROASTED VEGETABLES:

1 green bell pepper, seeded

1 onion, peeled

Olive oil, for drizzling

TO SERVE:

4 sub rolls

Gruyère cheese slices

Two L.A. restaurants claim invention of the French dip, and it is not known *oo is zee liar*. The first is Philippe's The Original, who claim the sandwich was created by Philippe Mathieu, who served it either because he a) dropped the sandwich in the meat juices but served it anyway; b) dipped it in the juices to satisfy a customer who hated wastage; or c) used it to disguise stale bread.

The second is Cole's Pacific Electric Buffet. Cole's claims the sandwich was invented when it was dipped to soften the bread for a customer suffering from, er, sore gums. Some soup instead, perhaps? Still others claim the sandwich was invented for the reasons stated by Philippe's but at Cole's Buffet. Both were established in 1908. In short, no one knows now and no one is ever likely to, unless there is a major increase in funding for time-travel research.

The French Dip

First make the beef broth (stock) for the gravy. Preheat the oven to 400°F (200°C) Gas 6.

Spread out the beef bones on a large baking sheet and roast them in the oven for about 30 minutes or until deep brown.

In a large stockpot, put all the remaining ingredients for the broth, including the roasted bones, and cover with water. Bring to a boil, skimming off the scum from the top as it rises. Reduce to a simmer and cook, partially-covered, for about 3 hours, skimming off the scum every now and then and topping up the water, if necessary.

Once cooked, remove from the heat, skim any fat from the surface, strain, and use the broth as required, or leave it to cool, then refrigerate until needed. Any leftover broth will keep in an airtight container in the refrigerator for up to 3 days or it can be frozen for up to 3 months.

To make the gravy, toss the cubed steak in flour to coat all over. Heat a little vegetable oil in a frying pan or skillet and brown the meat in batches. Transfer the browned meat to a saucepan, then cover with about 4¼ cups (1 liter) of the hot beef broth. Bring to a simmer, stirring, then simmer for an hour or more, until thick, reduced, and unctuous. Serve some of the cooked steak chunks in the gravy pot for dipping.

Meanwhile, roast the topside of beef. Preheat the oven to 400°F (200°C) Gas 6. Put the beef topside into a roasting pan and roast in the oven for about 1 hour for medium beef or until cooked to your liking. Remove from the oven, cover with aluminum foil, and let rest for 15–20 minutes before carving into slices.

While the beef is roasting, make the coleslaw. Mix all the ingredients together in a large bowl and season to taste with salt and pepper. Cover and chill in the refrigerator until ready to serve.

To serve, split and fill each roll with slices of hot roast beef and top with coleslaw, then serve with a pot of the gravy alongside.

COOK'S TIP:

The cooked chunks of steak will be utterly delicious served in the gravy pot for dipping.

Makes 8

INGREDIENTS

FOR THE BEEF BROTH (STOCK):

Fresh beef bones (about 6 large)

1 onion, halved

1 carrot, cut in half

2 celery stalks, cut into several large chunks

6 black peppercorns

A few fresh flat-leaf parsley stalks

2 bay leaves, torn

FOR THE GRAVY AND ROAST BEEF:

1lb 2oz (500g) cubed steak (stewing steak), cut into 1in (2.5cm) cubes

All-purpose (plain) flour, for dusting

Vegetable oil, for frying

1¾lb (800g) piece of beef topside

FOR THE COLESLAW:

2 carrots, cut into short, very thin sticks

½ green (white) cabbage, very finely shredded

Juice of ½ lemon

1 tbsp creamed horseradish sauce, or to taste

1 tbsp snipped fresh chives

Sea salt and black pepper, to taste

8 soft white rolls, to serve

The Ultimate Chicken Sandwich

I created this sandwich after an indulgent dinner of "Chicken with 40 Cloves of Garlic." It was quickly named as "the best chicken sandwich of my life." A whole chicken is cooked with, you've guessed it, 40 cloves of garlic and a generous cup (250ml) of olive oil.

The oil that remains after cooking is mixed with the fat from the bird and is precious liquor. Here it is used to make an incredible garlic mayo. Together with the smooshed roasted garlic, the roast meat, and lettuce spiked with lemon, this really is the ultimate chicken sandwich.

To roast the chicken, first preheat the oven to 375°F (190°C) Gas 5.

Un-truss the chicken and remove all fat from the cavity (if you look just inside, there are two blobs, one on either side—cut them off). Drizzle a little olive oil over the whole chicken and rub it in.

Heat a large frying pan or skillet and use it to brown the chicken, whole, as best you can (it won't be browning in the oven, as it will be covered with aluminum foil). Place the chicken in a roasting pan and surround it with the garlic cloves, then add the sprigs of thyme and the bay leaves. Stick the other thyme sprigs and the lemon slices inside the cavity. Pour the olive oil around the chicken—don't be tempted to use less oil.

Season the chicken very generously with salt and pepper, then cover with foil and seal it tightly. Roast in the oven for 1½–2 hours, until cooked, basting it 2–3 times during cooking. The chicken is cooked when you insert a skewer into the thickest part of the leg and, when pressed gently, the juices run clear. The legs will also feel looser when the bird is cooked.

Remove from the oven and rest the bird with its legs in the air, covered with the foil, for about 15–20 minutes. Once rested, let the chicken and garlic cool completely, then refrigerate until you are ready to make the sandwiches (the roast chicken and garlic can, of course, be served hot, and then any leftovers can be used to make fewer sandwiches, if you prefer). The garlic-infused oil should be strained and then left to cool completely, before using it to make the mayo for the sandwiches.

Once the oil is cold, make your mayonnaise. Put the egg yolks in a clean bowl and whisk them together. Begin adding the garlic-infused oil a few drops at a time, whisking as you do so and making sure each bit of oil is fully incorporated before adding the next. As you whisk more oil in and the mayo starts to thicken, you can start adding the oil in slightly larger quantities until you are steadily adding it in a thin stream. The key with mayo is to be cautious with the oil until you get a feel for making it. If you add too much oil at once, the mixture will split (if this happens, don't despair; take a fresh egg yolk in a clean bowl and begin adding the split mixture into it, very slowly, just as if it were the oil—this should bring it back). Stop when the mayo reaches the desired thickness. Add lemon juice and salt and pepper, to taste.

Makes 6

INGREDIENTS

FOR THE CHICKEN WITH 40 CLOVES OF GARLIC:

**One 4½lb (2kg) good-quality
oven-ready chicken**

**Generous 1 cup (250ml) olive oil,
plus extra for drizzling**

**40 garlic cloves or thereabouts
(that's about 4 whole bulbs),
papery bits removed but not
peeled**

**2 sprigs of fresh thyme (plus
2 extra sprigs for the cavity)**

2 bay leaves

A couple of lemon slices

**Sea salt and black pepper,
to taste (and lots of it)**

FOR THE MAYO AND SANDWICHES:

2 large egg yolks

**Leftover cooled oil from the
roast chicken and garlic cloves
above**

Lemon juice, to taste

12 slices sourdough bread

**Curly endive or other bitter
salad leaves, to serve**

To assemble the sandwiches, remove all the chicken meat from the carcass (discard the bones or use them to make broth/stock) and then chop the meat into small dice.

Mix the mayo with the diced chicken meat, then heap the mixture onto 6 slices of the bread. Spread the roast garlic flesh (squeezed out of the skins) on the other bread slices. Add some curly endive or other bitter salad leaves, tossed with a generous amount of lemon juice and salt and pepper. Sandwich together and serve.

Shawarma

Kebabs have a somewhat tarnished reputation as poor-quality meat mops, sponging up the consequences of a boozy night out. Often referred to as an "elephant's leg," the great rotating kebab shop spit is regarded with derision during sobriety.

A proper shawarma, however, is something special. This Levantine-Arab specialty sees various types of meat, including beef, lamb, chicken, veal, or a mixture, marinated in a complex blend of herbs and spices, mounted on a spit, and broiled (grilled) vertically, ready to be shaved and served to order. The shawarma can also refer to sliced marinated meats, which are grilled over the direct heat of the fire.

As with many sandwiches, particularly spiced ones, condiments are key; the shawarma is usually served with parsley-flecked tabbouleh, tarator sauce (a tahini garlic sauce; every kebab shop has its secret recipe), pickles, and cooling cucumber and tomato.

To prepare the lamb and marinade, mix all the ingredients together, except the lamb and salt and pepper for seasoning. Make deep slits all over the lamb and spread the marinade all over it, working it into the meat. Cover and refrigerate overnight.

The next day, bring the lamb to room temperature. Light a BBQ for direct grilling. Once the flames have died down and the coals have turned white, it's ready for cooking. Season the lamb with salt and pepper. Place the lamb on the grill, fat-side down, and grill for about 20 minutes. Turn the lamb over and grill for a further 20 minutes, until cooked. Remove the lamb from the grill, cover with aluminum foil, and let rest for 15 minutes before slicing and serving.

Meanwhile, make the tarator sauce and tabbouleh salad.

To make the tarator sauce, mix all the ingredients together in a bowl, adding enough cold water to loosen the mixture to the consistency of ketchup. Season to taste with salt and pepper, then cover and refrigerate until ready to serve.

To make the tabbouleh, mix all the ingredients together and then season to taste with salt and pepper. Cover and refrigerate until ready to serve.

To assemble the sandwiches, toast the pita breads, then split and fill with hot sliced lamb, tarator sauce, tabbouleh, and sliced tomatoes, cucumber, and pickles. Serve at once.

Makes 10

INGREDIENTS

FOR THE LAMB AND MARINADE:

4 tbsp red wine vinegar

Finely grated zest and juice of 1 lemon

2 garlic cloves, crushed

1 tsp paprika

1 tsp ground cumin

1 tsp ground coriander

3 cardamom pods, crushed

Pinch of superfine (caster) sugar

At least 1 tsp black pepper

2 tbsp olive oil

5½lb (2.5kg) leg of lamb, butterflied

Sea salt and black pepper, to taste

FOR THE TARATOR SAUCE:

1 slice white bread (crusts removed), broken up into small pieces

1 tbsp tahini, or to taste

3 garlic cloves (skin on), roasted and cooled, then the soft flesh squeezed out of the skins

1 tbsp finely chopped fresh flat-leaf parsley

Generous pinch of ground cumin

FOR THE TABBOULEH:

⅓ cup (50g) bulgur wheat, cooked according to packet instructions, then drained and cooled

3oz (85g) fresh flat-leaf parsley leaves (a bit of stalk is fine), very finely chopped

6 cherry tomatoes, very finely chopped

4 scallions (spring onions), green parts only, very thinly sliced

A small handful of fresh mint leaves, very finely chopped

1 garlic clove (peeled), blanched for a minute in boiling water, then drained and crushed

About 4 tbsp olive oil

Lemon juice, to taste

10 large pita breads, to serve

Sliced tomatoes, cucumber, and pickles (pickled chilies and pickled turnips are ideal), to serve

Makes 8

INGREDIENTS
FOR THE BEEF FILLING:

5½lb (2.5kg) beef short ribs (also known as "Jacob's ladder")

All-purpose (plain) flour, for dusting

Sea salt and black pepper, to taste

Vegetable oil, for frying

2 celery stalks, cut into a few lengths

1 large onion, cut into wedges

2 carrots, cut into a few lengths

5 garlic cloves, peeled

2 bay leaves

A small sprig of fresh thyme

Pinch of crushed red pepper flakes (chili flakes)

A handful of dried apricots

Generous 1¼ cups (320ml) bourbon

3¾ cups (900ml) beef broth (stock)

FOR THE QUICK PICKLED ONIONS:

2 tbsp superfine (caster) sugar

1 tbsp sea salt

Generous 1 cup (250ml) cider vinegar

2 red onions, sliced

8 soft white rolls, to serve

Celery leaves, to garnish (optional)

Beef Short Rib Sandwich

Beef short ribs are known as 'Jacob's ladder' ribs. The bourbon and apricots in the sauce give it a Deep South feel, while the pickled onions give the rich sauce what for, so don't leave them out.

To make the beef filling, dust the beef ribs all over in flour seasoned with salt and pepper. Brown them in some hot vegetable oil in a large saucepan or stockpot until browned on all sides. Remove to a large plate and set aside. Next, brown the celery, onion, and carrot pieces in a little more oil (about 2 tbsp), then add the rest of the filling ingredients, scraping up the brown bits from the bottom of the pan. Add the ribs back to the pan, bone-side down. Bring to a boil, then cover, reduce the heat, and simmer for 1 hour.

Carefully turn the ribs over, re-cover, and simmer for a further hour, until very tender. Remove from the heat and let the ribs cool in the pan until the fat can be removed from the top of the mixture and discarded. Reserve the ribs and any juices left in the pan.

Meanwhile, as the ribs are cooking, make the quick pickled onions. Whisk the sugar, salt, and vinegar together in a bowl until the sugar and salt are completely dissolved. Add the red onion slices and stir, then let sit for a couple of hours or so at room temperature.

Remove the warm meat from the ribs and cut it into chunks, then mix with the reserved pan juices.

To serve, split the rolls, fill with the rib meat and juices, then drain the pickled onions and spoon on top. Garnish with celery leaves, if using.

Fried Chicken Sandwich

Whether Southern-fried, Kentucky-fried, or simple chicken nuggets, the chicken sure does make for some mighty fine eating once spice-coated and plunged into hot oil.

Makes 4

INGREDIENTS

FOR THE BRINE FOR THE CHICKEN:

1 tsp sea salt

1 tsp superfine (caster) sugar

1¼ cups (300ml) buttermilk

4 skinless, boneless chicken breasts (each about 6oz/175g)

FOR THE SEASONED FLOUR:

Scant 1¼ cups (150g) all-purpose (plain) flour

1½ tsp black pepper

1 tsp smoked paprika

½ tsp cayenne pepper

1 tsp garlic powder

1 tsp onion powder

1 tsp celery seeds

1 tsp superfine (caster) sugar

2 tsp sea salt

Peanut (groundnut) oil, for deep-frying

4 soft white rolls, split open

Mayonnaise

Shredded iceberg lettuce

To make the brine solution for the chicken, mix the salt, sugar, and buttermilk together in a bowl. Submerge the chicken breasts in this buttermilk-brine mixture, then cover and refrigerate for 8 hours. The next day, when you are ready to cook, allow the chicken to come back to room temperature before cooking it.

To make the seasoned flour, mix the flour and all the other ingredients together in a wide shallow dish. Take a couple of tablespoonfuls of the buttermilk-brine mixture from the chicken and sprinkle it into the seasoned flour, mixing it about. This will help to create a more craggy surface on the finished fried chicken.

Heat some peanut (groundnut) oil in a large, heavy-based frying pan or skillet to a depth of ¾in (2cm) and to a temperature of 350°F (180°C).

Wipe as much of the buttermilk-brine mixture from the chicken as possible using paper towels, and then dip each breast into the seasoned flour, coating well all over. Cook the chicken in the hot oil for about 5–6 minutes on each side, turning once, until golden and cooked through (the cooking time will depend on the thickness of the chicken breasts).

Drain the chicken breasts on a rack set over some paper towels.

Lightly toast the rolls, then generously spread the bottom half of each one with mayo. Top each one with some lettuce, a hot fried chicken breast, and then the other half of the roll. Serve now!

Tunisian Fricassee Sandwich

The Tunisian fricassee has one serious trump card to play over some of the other sandwiches in this book and that is the fact that the bread dough is fried. The idea of plunging things into hot oil should never be dismissed without proper consideration. The main filling ingredients here—tuna, eggs, potatoes, capers—may seem more fitting with something like a Pan Bagnat (see recipe on page 94), but the exotic curveball comes in the form of the chili paste, harissa, and the intoxicating perfume of preserved lemons.

Makes 10

INGREDIENTS
FOR THE FRICASSEE ROLLS:

1 tsp superfine (caster) sugar

1 tsp sea salt

1 egg

2 cups (250g) all-purpose (plain) flour

About 1 tsp easy-blend dried yeast

Scant ½–⅔ cup (100–150ml) warm water

Vegetable oil, for deep-frying

FOR THE ISRAELI SALAD:

2 ripe tomatoes, very finely chopped

1 small cucumber, very finely chopped

½ red onion, very finely chopped

½ green bell pepper, seeded and very finely chopped

A handful of fresh flat-leaf parsley leaves, very finely chopped

Juice of ½ lemon, or to taste

Sea salt and black pepper, to taste

A splash of olive oil

FOR THE FILLINGS:

Harissa, to taste

5 x 6½oz (185g) cans good-quality tuna, drained and flaked

5 cold hard-boiled eggs, peeled and sliced

20 whole pitted (stoned) black olives

1lb 2oz (500g) cooked potatoes, sliced

2 tbsp capers, rinsed and patted dry

1 preserved lemon, drained and finely chopped

To make the fricassee rolls, mix together the sugar, salt, and egg. In a large mixing bowl, combine the flour and yeast. Add the egg mixture, then gradually add enough warm water, mixing until you have a soft, stretchy dough. Knead for about 5 minutes, then place the dough in a clean oiled bowl, cover with a clean dish towel, and let rise in a warm place for about 1 hour, until doubled in size.

Once risen, gently punch down (knock back) the dough and knead again for a few minutes. Divide the dough into 10 pieces, then shape each one into an elongated roll shape. Place on a baking sheet lined with wax (greaseproof) paper, cover, and let rise again in a warm place for about 45 minutes, until doubled in size.

While the dough is proving (rising), make the Israeli salad. Mix all the vegetables, the parsley, and lemon juice together and season with salt and pepper. Add more lemon juice, if desired, and mix in a splash of olive oil. Cover and refrigerate until ready to serve.

Once the rolls are ready to cook, pour some vegetable oil into a deep frying pan or an electric deep-fat fryer and heat to 350°F (180°C). Deep-fry the rolls in batches for a few minutes on each side, turning once, until golden all over and cooked through. Drain on paper towels and keep warm in a low oven while you cook the rest.

To assemble the sandwiches, split the warm rolls, spread with harissa to taste, then layer on the tuna, eggs, olives, potatoes, a sprinkle of capers, and a helping of Israeli salad. Garnish with a few pieces of preserved lemon and serve.

Ham and Mustard Sandwich

Makes 10

The key to this sandwich is simplicity. The most important element is a good-quality ham on the bone, home roasted. The only condiments necessary are salted butter and nostril-clearing mustard.

INGREDIENTS

6lb (2.7kg) bone-in joint of ham (check with your butcher whether or not the ham needs soaking, if it does, ask for how long, as this will depend on the salt content)

Whole cloves

Scant ¼ cup (50g) light brown packed sugar

3 tbsp whole-grain mustard

10 soft white rolls, split open

Butter, at room temperature

English mustard, to serve

Once the ham is soaked (if necessary) and ready to cook, preheat the oven to 325°F (170°C) Gas 3. Line a baking pan with aluminum foil in both directions, crosswise and lengthwise, so that you are able to then place the ham in the center, and pull the foil up around it to make a tent. Cook the ham in the oven for 2 hours.

Remove the ham from the oven and carefully unwrap it. Turn the oven temperature up to 400°F (200°C) Gas 6. Carefully remove the skin from the ham, taking care to leave as much fat behind as possible. Score the fat all over into diamond shapes, then stud each diamond with a clove. Mix the sugar and whole-grain mustard together in a bowl and then rub it all over the ham. Cook in the oven for a further 30 minutes, until glazed and nice and sticky.

Remove from the oven, cover with clean foil, and let the ham rest for about 30 minutes before slicing; I know… it's hard.

Serve the warm ham slices in the white rolls with plenty of butter and English mustard—as much as your sinuses can handle.

The Cuban Sandwich

The Cuban sandwich, or "cubano" hails from, you've guessed it, Cuba, but it quickly became popular in the southeast United States, specifically Florida, where many Cuban immigrants settled to work in cigar factories. A standard cubano consists of mojo-roasted pork, sliced ham, cheese, pickles, and mustard, plus an added topping of controversy over whether or not a "true" version should contain salami.

This sandwich should ideally be made with Cuban bread, which is enriched with lard and is notable for the way it toasts into a very crisp, flat sandwich. Cuban bread can be tricky to find, so a baguette or panini-style bread can be substituted.

Start the pork the day before you want to eat it. If the meat has a thick layer of fat, make some scores in it so the marinade can penetrate. With a pestle and mortar, pound together the garlic, salt, a decent amount of black pepper, and the cumin seeds. Mix in the oregano.

Place the pork in a non-reactive dish and smear the garlic-oregano mixture all over it. Mix together the onion, the citrus zests and juices, and a good glug of olive oil and pour this over the pork. Turn the pork over in the marinade, then cover and refrigerate overnight, turning occasionally (if you're awake).

The next day, preheat the oven to 300°F (150°C) Gas 2. Transfer the pork and marinade to a roasting pan, cover with aluminum foil, and roast in the oven for 2 hours, basting occasionally. Remove the foil and roast the pork for a further 1½ hours, until the meat is fork-tender and the top is browned. If it gets too brown, replace the foil. You may also need to add a little water during cooking if the pan gets too dry.

When the meat is cooked, remove it from the oven, cover with clean foil, and let rest for at least 30 minutes, before slicing and serving. If you do find that the roasting juices have caramelized too much, try adding some warm water and stirring to reconstitute the sauce.

To assemble the sandwiches, cut each Cuban roll almost in half lengthwise, leaving a join along one side. Brush the crust lightly with olive oil, then spread the top half of each roll with Dijon mustard. On the bottom half of each roll, layer on some of the roast pork and the roasting juices. Add 2 slices of ham, followed by 1 slice of cheese, top with some dill pickle slices, then add the top half of each roll.

Heat a skillet or frying pan (or a panini press, if you have one) and melt some butter in it. Add a sandwich to the skillet (cook 1 sandwich at a time). Press the sandwich down and then weight it down with another heavy skillet placed on top, so that it is about one-third of its original thickness. Cook until golden, then turn over and toast the other side until golden. Cut in half diagonally and serve. Cook and serve the remaining sandwiches in the same way.

Makes 10

INGREDIENTS

FOR THE PORK:

4½lb (2kg) boneless pork shoulder

10 garlic cloves, peeled

1 heaped tbsp sea salt

Black pepper, to taste

½ tsp cumin seeds

2 tsp dried oregano

1 onion, grated

Finely grated zest of 1 orange

Finely grated zest of 1 lime

⅔ cup (150ml) freshly squeezed orange juice

Scant ⅓ cup (80ml) freshly squeezed lime juice

Olive oil

10 Cuban-style bread rolls (or a baguette or panini-style bread if no Cuban bakers are to hand)

Dijon mustard, to taste

20 cooked ham slices

10 Swiss cheese slices

3 dill pickles (pickled gherkins), drained and sliced, or to taste

Butter

Frittata Sandwich

Makes 1 frittata; serves 6

INGREDIENTS

Vegetable oil, for frying

1 large onion, sliced

1 red bell pepper, seeded and sliced

1 yellow bell pepper, seeded and sliced

6 eggs

½ tsp smoked paprika

1 heaped tbsp snipped fresh chives

Sea salt and black pepper, to taste

7oz (200g) (or as much as you like) goat's cheese (with rind left on), sliced

Sliced bread of your choice, to make sandwiches from the leftovers

Ketchup and hot chili sauce, to serve

One could, of course, use any flavors in this sandwich; the world is your frittata. Personally, I favor the sweetness of bell peppers and onions, which also give a lovely texture and match well with one of the best sauces for leftover sandwiches: ketchup and hot chili sauce mixed together (don't judge me).

I'm sure, too, that by this point in the book I do not need to remind readers to ALWAYS CONSIDER DOUBLE CARBS. The possibility of using that leftover Spanish frittata (or a potato and egg combo of any other nationality) as a filling should never be dismissed.

Preheat the broiler (grill) to medium.

Heat some vegetable oil in a large, ovenproof skillet or frying pan and gently cook the onion and bell peppers until softened and starting to color. Crack all the eggs into a bowl and beat together lightly with the smoked paprika and chives, plus some salt and pepper. Pour into the skillet, spreading the mixture around so it is roughly even on top. Press the slices of goat's cheese all over the top and garnish with a little extra black pepper.

Cook the frittata over a low to moderate heat until you can see the edges have cooked, then pop it under the broiler for 4–5 minutes to finish cooking on top. Be careful to watch it at this stage, as it can burn easily.

Remove from the heat and serve hot, cut into wedges, or let go cold, then serve any leftovers in a sandwich bread of your choice, with a sauce made by mixing together ketchup and hot chili sauce, to taste. If you prefer, the frittata wedges can simply be served hot in the sandwiches.

Refrigerator Buffet Sandwich

The concept of the refrigerator buffet sandwich was defined by my friend and pub landlord extraordinaire, Oisin Rogers. It basically involves a late-night raid on the refrigerator, but I feel it is best explained by the man himself, thus:

"It is most likely to occur at around two in the morning. Items from the refrigerator, freezer, and pantry are allowed, including leftovers. The matching of stuff depends often on the extent to which the muses have swept away my senses. Self-imposed law forbids the use of electrical or mains gas appliances, except the fridge and the freezer.

"Refrigerator Buffet began to become interesting from the weird food aisle at the supermarket. I began to have a slightly different vista when in ethnic or specialist food stores. I might spot a jar or can of something. Anchovy paste, Kimchi, No. 5 Umami, confiture du caramel, harissa, chipotle, kerda pickle, or salted galangal. These become coveted purchases, for my late night gluttonous armory."

Osh says he prefers the ballast of a crispbread or cracker. I, of course, would shovel everything between two slices of bread.

To the left are some of Osh's combinations but, of course, the sandwich should consist of whatever can be foraged from the refrigerator. The buffet should always come with a drink, preferably alcoholic.

Makes 1

INGREDIENTS

Fillings of your choice, foraged from the refrigerator (see some of Osh's combinations below)

2 slices bread of your choice

▪ Lettuce, sun-dried tomatoes, brined cockles, capers, rouille. Dessert: blood orange, mint sugar. Drink: Amaretto sour.

▪ Doritos, anchovy paste, green tomato jam, aged Gouda, saucisson, baby capers. Dessert: melon, honey. Drink: PX sherry.

▪ Ispíni, green tomato and Tabasco or hot chili sauce, focaccia. Drink: Innis & Gunn beer.

Roast Dinner Sandwich

This one does what it says on the tin, really; it's all the best leftover bits from a classic Sunday roast. I mean the scraps one digs deep for: the caramelized edge bits on the roasted meat, the crispiest potatoes left at the bottom of the roasting pan, the stickiest smear of gravy... The ingredients here obviously depend on what you cooked in the first place, so this really is just a guide.

Smoosh the roast potatoes onto 1 slice of bread, then layer up the meat and vegetables on top. Spread the other slice of bread with your sauce of choice. Drizzle the meat and vegetables with a little gravy, if desired, and sandwich together.

Devour, and marvel at how it was worth cooking a whole roast just to make this sandwich happen.

Makes 1

INGREDIENTS

A couple of leftover roast potatoes

2 slices sturdy bread

Slices of leftover roast meat, my favorite being some pork belly with lots of lovely leftover crackling

Some leftover vegetables, in the case of roast pork, some cabbage would work well

An appropriate sauce, e.g. apple sauce in the case of roast pork, mint sauce for lamb, horseradish sauce for beef

Leftover gravy, perhaps (can be reheated if you like)

Dripping Sandwich

Dripping is animal fat, usually cow, and it is tasty. In the home it is collected from the residues of roasted meat, although it's used in larger quantities in fish and chip shops, where it is sometimes used to fry chips in place of oil. The fat has taken on all the flavor of the meat and as such used to be highly prized as a sandwich spread.

This is a true British classic, which is losing popularity. This is, quite frankly, a crime, and should be punishable by law. It's time to revive the dripping (or, as they say in Yorkshire, "mucky fat") sandwich.

Spread the dripping over 1 slice of bread, then sprinkle with salt and pepper. Top with the other slice of bread. Serve at once.

Makes 1

INGREDIENTS

Dripping harvested from the roasting pan used to cook a piece of beef

2 slices bread

Sea salt and black pepper, to taste

We can all make a grilled or toasted cheese sandwich, and pretty much everyone makes their own variation, which is why this recipe focuses on ways to pimp the basic version. Of course, if you own a sandwich toaster, you'd be a fool not to use it (apparently the toastie machine is one of the most neglected kitchen gadgets—completely baffling), but a toasted cheese sandwich can also be made in a frying pan or skillet. I give the latter method here.

Pimp Your Toasted Cheese Sandwich

Spread both slices of bread generously with butter. Take 1 slice of bread and cover it very enthusiastically with GRATED cheese on the un-buttered side. This is a toasted cheese sandwich—it is never going to be healthy. Add your pimpage of choice and then the other slice of bread, buttered-side up.

Heat a heavy-based frying pan or skillet and melt a little butter in it. Put the sandwich into the frying pan, then weight it down with another heavy pan placed on top, and cook until golden and crisp on the bottom. Flip and repeat. Briefly flip to the original side for 30 seconds or so to make sure it is hot on both sides. Drain on paper towels and serve at once.

WAYS TO PIMP YOUR TOASTED CHEESE SANDWICH:

- Hot chili sauce; either in the sandwich or on the side.
- Sliced scallions (spring onions); rarely is there a sandwich that cannot be improved by the addition of scallions. This is an absolute truth. Cheese and onion is a classic combination and on that note...
- Several types of onion (sliced). Different onions have different flavors and when combined they can be wonderful; consider using sweet red onions, the more intense regular onions, and scallions (spring onions) all together.

And before I'm done on the onion tip... caramelized onions are wonderful, particularly when cooked with a splash of beer, brandy, or whiskey.
- Crisp cooked bacon bits.
- Salami or cooked chorizo.
- Fresh or pickled sliced jalapeños.
- Sautéed mushrooms.
- Kimchi (kimchi is a dish of fermented cabbage, Chinese leaves, or other vegetables, flavored with ground Korean chili).
- Chutney.

INGREDIENTS

FOR THE BASIC TOASTED CHEESE SANDWICH:

**2 slices sourdough bread
(ideally a couple of days
old; very fresh sourdough
can go a little greasy
when toasted)**

**Butter, at room
temperature**

**Cheese of your choice,
grated—melting cheeses
such as Gruyère or other
Swiss cheese, Cheddar,
Raclette, Fontina, or
Taleggio all work well**

**Your choice of pimpage
from the list opposite**

Christmas Sandwich 1

For me, the Christmas dinner leftovers sandwich is better than the meal itself. What is it about stuffing everything between two slices of bread that improves it so? Of course, all the components have had time to sit and mature, making them even tastier than they once were. It's also possible to get a lot more textural contrast and flavor in just one bite.

Once the ingredients are cold, it opens up options on the condiment front, such as chutneys and pickles, which wouldn't have been appropriate with a hot meal. It is able to deal with leftover Christmas cheese. The list of benefits is endless.

This is my personal favorite combination for a Christmas sandwich, followed by another one, which I'm almost too ashamed to admit to making. Almost.

Makes 1

INGREDIENTS

Leftover cooked turkey meat, preferably brown

Leftover pigs in blankets (sausages wrapped in bacon)

Leftover stuffing

Cheese, sliced, such as Stilton, Brie, or Camembert

Pickled onions, drained and sliced

Mayonnaise

A few token lettuce leaves, for greenery and crunch

2 thick slices white bread

Layer everything up between the slices of bread to make your sandwich. Open wide and chow down on this seasonal beast.

Christmas Sandwich 2

My other favorite Christmas sandwich. Could be in the guilty pleasure section, this one...

Layer up all the ingredients between the bread slices to make your sandwich. Tuck on in. Don't feel a shred of guilt—it's Christmas.

Makes 1

INGREDIENTS

Sliced pork pie

Leftover sliced cooked ham (the thick, clove-studded kind)

Piccalilli

2 thick slices white bread

Student's Zapiekanka

The Polish Zapiekanka sneaks in here as another open-faced sandwich. It comes hot and topped with cheese and mushrooms, plus different types of meat, vegetables, and sauce, depending on what leftovers are available at the time. The student version is even more flexible, not requiring the usually necessary mushroom element, but just leftover bread and cheese, plus whatever can be found in the house. Well, in the kitchen, at least.

Heat a little vegetable oil in a frying pan or skillet and gently cook the red onion, bell pepper, and mushrooms until soft and starting to color. Add the jalapeños and olives and cook gently, stirring, for a few minutes more, until heated through.

Preheat the broiler (grill) to high.

Take each baguette half and scoop out some of the crumb to make a "bread boat" shape, then heap some of the filling into each half and top with a good layer of cheese. Toast under the broiler until the cheese is bubbling and golden. Serve at once with ketchup.

Makes 1

INGREDIENTS

Vegetable oil, for frying

1 red onion, chopped

1 red or green bell pepper, seeded and chopped

6 button mushrooms, sliced

2 pickled jalapeño chilies, drained and chopped

A handful of pitted (stoned) black olives, sliced

½ baguette, cut in half lengthwise

Grated cheese of your choice, for melting

Ketchup, to serve

The Moistmaker

This isn't so much a sandwich recipe as a technique, invented by the character Monica Geller in the comedy series "Friends," and beloved of her brother, Ross. It consists of a layer of bread in the center of a sandwich, which has been dipped in gravy, therefore keeping the sandwich lovely and moist. There is an episode in which someone steals Ross's Thanksgiving leftover sandwich, complete with moistmaker, from his shared workplace refrigerator. He is suitably unimpressed.

Makes 1

INGREDIENTS

3 slices whole-wheat (brown) bread

Mayonnaise

Whole lettuce leaves (something soft like an English or butterhead lettuce would be good here)

Leftover roast turkey slices

Leftover cold gravy

Leftover stuffing

Cranberry sauce

Spread 1 slice of the bread with mayonnaise. Add a layer of lettuce, then a layer of roast turkey. Dip a second slice of bread in gravy and lay it on top. Follow with a layer of stuffing. Spread the final slice of bread with cranberry sauce and lay it on top to complete your sandwich. Serve at once.

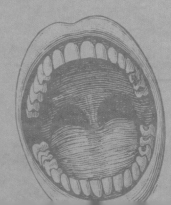

Haslet Sandwich

Haslet is a British meatloaf from Lincolnshire made from ground pork mince and herbs. In effect, it's like a coarse pâté and, as such, is lovely eaten in a sandwich complemented by some nose-searing English mustard, as much as your sinuses can handle.

To make the meatloaf, preheat the oven to 350°F (180°C) Gas 4.

Soak the 4 thick bread slices in enough milk just to cover for about 5 minutes, then squeeze out the excess milk. Mix the soaked bread with all the other meatloaf ingredients. Pack the meatloaf mixture into a 1lb (450g) loaf pan, cover with aluminum foil, and cook in the oven for about 1 hour, until cooked through, removing the foil about 15 minutes before the end of the cooking time.

Remove from the oven, then let cool in the pan for a couple of hours or so, before turning out (see Cook's Tip). Wrap in foil, store in the refrigerator, and use within 3 days.

To make the sandwiches, slice the cold meatloaf and then sandwich it between slices of bread spread with English mustard. Serve with cornichons—the cornichons can be sliced and served in the sandwiches, or simply served alongside.

Makes 1 meatloaf; serves 6

INGREDIENTS
FOR THE MEATLOAF:

4 thick slices white bread, crusts removed

Milk

10½oz (300g) coarsely ground (minced) pork belly

5½oz (150g) pig's liver, chopped

1 onion, finely chopped

1 scant tbsp dried sage

Pinch of ground nutmeg

Sea salt and black pepper, to taste

FOR THE SANDWICHES:

Sliced bread of your choice

English mustard

Cornichons, to serve

COOK'S TIP:

If you would like to serve the haslet hot (and then serve any leftovers cold in sandwiches), let the cooked meatloaf pan cool in the tin for about 30 minutes before turning out and slicing.

This is my competition-winning macaroni and cheese recipe, no less. This means it is going to take some time to make, but the good news is that the results are well worth the effort. Not only will you be rewarded with kick ass mac 'n' cheese, you will revel in the kind of smugness that can only come from creating one of the best leftovers sandwiches ever.

The key to this recipe is the inclusion of ham hock, which is simmered with aromatics, creating an incredible ham broth (stock); this is then used to cook the macaroni. The pieces of shredded ham are mixed in with the pasta and two types of cheese to create the ultimate mac daddy.

When pressed and grilled between two slices of bread, the cheese reheats and becomes oozy once again, a gooey mass studded with porky pieces nonetheless. Oh and let's not forget how good macaroni cheese tastes the day after it's made...

Mac 'n' Cheese Sandwich

To cook the ham hock, place it in a large saucepan with all the other ingredients for the ham hock and cover with water. Bring to a boil, then reduce the heat and simmer, uncovered, for about 2 hours, until cooked, topping up the water every now and then. Strain the broth (stock) into a bowl and reserve it for cooking the pasta. Discard the flavorings and flake the meat from the bone, taking care to avoid any bits of skin or sinew. Chop the meat into bite-size chunks and reserve for mixing into the mac.

Meanwhile, make the Mornay sauce and cook the macaroni. Melt the butter in a saucepan over a gentle heat and then add the flour, stirring quite vigorously to form a thick paste (or roux). Let this cook for a few minutes, stirring the whole time. Begin adding the milk, a little at a time, stirring constantly and making sure it is incorporated fully before adding more. Toward the end, you can start pouring in larger amounts. Add the nutmeg and cook over a low heat, stirring, for about 5 minutes. When it starts to thicken, add the Cheddar cheeses and stir until melted. Remove from the heat and season to taste with white pepper. If you need to keep it to one side, cover the surface with a piece of wax (greaseproof) paper to stop a skin forming.

In the meantime, cook the macaroni, according to the packet instructions, in the reserved ham broth, topping up with a little boiling water, if necessary.

To assemble and cook the mac, preheat the oven to 400°F (200°C) Gas 6. Mix the Mornay sauce with the cooked macaroni and ham hock pieces, then check the seasoning, adding more white pepper and a little salt, if necessary. Pile the mixture into a suitable well-buttered ovenproof dish. Sprinkle the breadcrumb and cheese mixture evenly over the top, grating a bit more cheese on top, if desired. Bake in the oven for about 30 minutes, until golden brown and crisp. Serve hot, if desired, and then keep any leftovers (in the refrigerator) to make delicious sandwiches—see opposite.

To make a Mac 'n' Cheese Sandwich

Spread the bread slices with lots of butter. Take 1 slice of the buttered bread and cover it very generously with leftover macaroni and cheese on the un-buttered side. Add the second slice of bread on top, buttered-side up.

Heat a heavy-based frying pan or skillet and melt a little butter in it. Put the sandwich into the frying pan and then weight it down with another heavy pan placed on top, and cook until golden and crisp on the bottom. Flip and repeat. Briefly flip to the original side for 30 seconds or so to make sure it is hot on both sides. Drain on paper towels and serve at once.

Makes 6

INGREDIENTS

FOR THE HAM HOCK:

1 ham hock, about 2¼lb (1kg)

1 bay leaf

6 black peppercorns

A few fresh flat-leaf parsley stalks

1 carrot, halved

1 celery stalk (stick), halved

1 onion, halved and studded with a couple of whole cloves

FOR THE MORNAY SAUCE, MACARONI, AND TOPPING:

½ stick (60g) butter

½ cup (60g) all-purpose (plain) flour

2¾ cups (650ml) milk

A swift grating of nutmeg (optional)

2¼ cups (250g) grated mature Cheddar cheese

Scant 1 cup (100g) grated smoked Cheddar cheese

White pepper and sea salt, to taste

12oz (350g) dried macaroni

Panko (or regular fresh) breadcrumbs (enough to cover), mixed with a good couple of handfuls of grated mature Cheddar cheese (when I made this, I grated a bit more on top and added a bit of grated Parmesan too, simply because I had it lying around, but that's optional)

FOR EACH SANDWICH:

2 slices sourdough bread or farmhouse white bread

Butter, at room temperature

Ice Cream Sandwich

What's better than ice cream? An ice cream sandwich, that's what. If you never made ice cream sandwiches as a kid, it doesn't matter because you're never too old to appreciate them. There are so many possible variations on this, including different flavored cookies and ice cream, wafers, biscuits, and extra bits and bobs like chocolate sprinkles, sugar sprinkles, (hundreds and thousands), and even a pot of sauce for dipping. Go wild, you crazy kid.

The recipe for this sandwich couldn't be easier. Simply sandwich the ice cream between the 2 cookies, add your extra ingredients of choice, and, voilà, it's ready to eat!

Makes 1

INGREDIENTS

2 scoops vanilla ice cream

2 chocolate chip cookies

Your choice of extra ingredients
(see below)

FIVE WAYS TO PIMP YOUR ICE CREAM SANDWICH:

- Mix up the flavors—chocolate and mint, vanilla and coffee, salted caramel and banana will all work a treat.
- Roll the edges of the ice cream in chopped nuts, colored sprinkles (hundreds and thousands), or chocolate sprinkles. If you want a super-indulgent cookie explosion, you could even roll the ice cream in chopped-up Oreos.
- Spread a layer of Nutella or your favorite fruit jelly (jam) onto the cookies before adding your ice cream.
- Serve a sauce such as chocolate or caramel on the side for dunking.
- Use slices of cake or wafers in place of cookies.

P. B. & J.

The peanut butter and jelly sandwich is a staple of the American schoolchild's lunchbox. Apparently the original flavor of "jelly" used was grape, which seems rather baffling to the non-US palate. You'll struggle to find grape jelly in many supermarkets outside of the States, so if you love it, stock up!

Makes 1

INGREDIENTS

2 slices white bread

Peanut butter (crunchy or smooth, the choice is yours)

Jelly (jam) of your choice (strawberry works well)

Spread 1 slice of bread with peanut butter, and the other slice with jelly (jam). Sandwich together and serve.

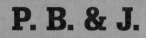

Sprinkles Sandwich

Australians may favor the multicolored disco sandwich that is "fairy bread," but the real champions of the sprinkles sandwich are the Dutch. They favor chocolate sprinkles (the word "sprinkles" in Dutch, "hagelslag," rather endearingly translates into English as "hailstorm") sandwiched between white bread. It's crunchy, it's sweet, and it seems just a little bit wrong, which, of course, makes it all the more enjoyable.

Spread 1 slice of bread with butter and cover with sprinkles, as desired. Add the other slice of bread to make a sandwich. Serve.

Makes 1

INGREDIENTS

2 slices white bread

Butter, at room temperature

Sprinkles, of your choice

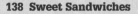

Nutella Sandwich

I thought Nutella was vile as a child, but it seems I was very much in the minority. I took one taste, screwed up my little face, and have carefully avoided it from then on. As an adult, I have learned the error of my ways. The chocolate hazelnut spread has been outrageously successful since its creation by a man named Pietro Ferrero in 1963, and is now sold in 75 countries. So, this sandwich is included for the masses.

I've heard that such sandwiches can be embellished with sliced banana, jelly (jam), or, I've just been informed by a friend as I write this, grated fresh coconut.

Toast the bread slices, then spread liberally with Nutella. Sprinkle with salt, if you like. Sandwich together and serve.

Makes 1

INGREDIENTS

2 slices bread (the choice is yours, although I imagine ciabatta would work rather well)

Nutella

Sea salt, to taste (optional)

Fluffernutter

The fluffernutter is so uniquely all-American, that people elsewhere may never have heard of it. The sandwich consists of that sweet sandwich staple, peanut butter, mixed with the slightly unnerving jarred cotton-like substance that is "marshmallow fluff." Insanely sticky and sweet, this substance is like whipped clouds in a pot.

The temptation to plunge finger into pot is overwhelming, but be warned, this extraordinary substance makes hands tacky like nothing else. It also has an unnerving ability to reform to its original shape over time, even though you'd never see it moving if you were to stare at the open pot for hours. It was invented by a man called Archibald Query, who sold the idea to two war veterans; they later went on to make the fluff stuff famous.

Makes 1

INGREDIENTS

2 slices white bread (the cheap "plasticy" kind works best)

Peanut butter (crunchy or smooth, the choice is yours)

Marshmallow fluff (also called marshmallow creme)—available from various outlets, including some supermarkets, grocery stores, and online

Spread 1 slice of bread with peanut butter and spread the other slice with marshmallow fluff. Do not attempt to spread one on top of the other; this never works. Sandwich together and eat, with sticky fingers.

Fruit and Nut Sandwich

We're more familiar with fruit and nut chocolate bars than sandwiches, but this is a recipe that crops up in old British cookbooks from the early 1900s. It's a nice idea, I think, and makes an interesting addition to an afternoon tea spread.

For a really fantastic variation on a more savory note, try a combination of fresh figs and goat's cheese.

Scoop out the soft flesh from the figs and mix it with the chopped dates and pecans. Spread onto 1 slice of bread.

Butter the other slice of bread and sandwich them together. Cut the crusts off and serve.

Makes 1

INGREDIENTS

2 large fresh ripe figs, cut in half

A few dried pitted (stoned) dates, finely chopped

A few pecans, finely chopped

2 large slices white bread

Butter, at room temperature

Scented Sandwich

The scented sandwich is another old English recipe, which involves covering the bread and butter with edible fresh flowers overnight, where they impart a subtle scent.

These are delicate-tasting sandwiches, as the name implies. They can be made with any edible flower, though "edible" is clearly the operative word here. Rose, nasturtium, and violet are all lovely choices.

Scented sandwiches are not particularly sweet, but their fragrance definitely makes them somewhat so, hence the inclusion here. A flowery sandwich must come under the category of dessert, surely.

Butter 1 slice of bread, lay the petals or flowers on it, then butter the second slice of bread and sandwich them together. Cover and leave in a cool place overnight.

In the morning, remove and discard the flowers, except for a few petals to grace the inside of the sandwich. Remove the crusts and cut into fingers, then serve.

Makes 1

INGREDIENTS

Butter, at room temperature

2 slices white bread

Edible fresh rose petals, nasturtiums or violets

Japanese Fruit Sandwich

Strawberries and cream, in a sandwich? Surely invented by the British? The answer is no. It's a popular sandwich filling in Japan, and is, in fact, made with any seasonal fruit, including kiwi and blueberries.

Spread 1 slice of bread generously with the whipped cream. Top with the sliced strawberries and then the second slice of bread.

Cut off the crusts and then cut the sandwich into neat shapes (such as fingers or triangles), trimming the sides, as necessary. Serve at once.

Makes 1

INGREDIENTS

2 slices soft white bread

Heavy whipping cream (whipped to stiff peaks with a little confectioners' (icing) sugar, to taste

5–6 fresh strawberries, hulled and sliced (or other fruit of your choice)

Sugar Sandwich

Sugar sandwiches, I'm sure, have provided a sweet fix for the hard up for donkey's years; I know they certainly did for people of a certain generation. Consisting of just two ingredients, sugar and bread, this is quite the experience. Limit consumption for tooth preservation.

Spread 1 slice of bread with butter, if you like. Sprinkle the sugar onto the buttered bread as liberally as desired. Sandwich together with the second slice of bread and eat.

Makes 1

INGREDIENTS

2 slices cheap white bread

Butter, at room temperature (optional)

Sugar—superfine (caster) sugar or light brown sugar is suitable

Monte Cristo Sandwich

The Monte Cristo seems to be confused. On the one hand it is a grilled meat and cheese sandwich—nothing unusual there. Then it is dipped in egg and fried; again, not particularly groundbreaking, but... wait a minute... it's finished with a dusting of confectioners' (icing) sugar and served with blackberry jelly (jam)?! Insane.

I love how this sandwich really gives the finger to healthy eating in every way possible. Melted cheese, tick! Fried in butter, tick! Dusted with sugar and dipped in jelly? Tick, and indeed, tick!

Makes 1

INGREDIENTS

3 slices white bread

Butter, at room temperature

2 slices cooked ham

2 slices cooked chicken or turkey

2 slices Gouda cheese

2 eggs, beaten

Splash of milk

Confectioners' (icing) sugar, for dusting

Blackberry jelly (jam), to serve

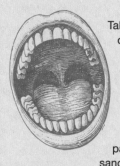

Take 1 slice of bread and butter it. Top with a slice of ham, a slice of chicken, and, finally, a slice of cheese. Butter a second slice of bread and add it to the sandwich, followed by the other slices of ham, chicken, and cheese. Butter the remaining slice of bread and use it to top the sandwich.

In a wide bowl, beat together the eggs with a good splash of milk. Melt some butter in a frying pan or skillet over a medium-high heat. Dip the sandwich into the egg mixture, coating both sides, then cook the sandwich in the frying pan until golden and crisp on both sides, turning once.

Drain on paper towels, then dust the hot sandwich with confectioners' (icing) sugar and serve with some blackberry jelly (jam).

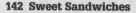

Index